# Trade Secrets:

# Tips, Tools and Timesavers
# for Primary and Elementary Teachers

## Second Edition

Billie J. Enz
Sharon A. Kortman
and
Connie J. Honaker

Arizona State University

**KENDALL/HUNT PUBLISHING COMPANY**
4050 Westmark Drive     Dubuque, Iowa 52002

# TABLE OF CONTENTS

# FOREWORD

The first day, week, month and year of school are simultaneously exciting and overwhelming; rewarding and frustrating; energizing and exhausting. These are all normal responses to the demands being placed on you as an educator. This text is designed to provide explicit information about the demands, decisions and details you will deal with in your teaching. Trade Secrets is organized into five major sections that parallel the concerns of teachers as they progress through the school year.

Section I: Starting the Year Successfully - focuses on the basics of understanding and fitting into the professional community. This section also details the specific procedures and routines for establishing a well-organized classroom.

Section II: Building Classroom Community - features information for proactively managing student behavior, communicating with parents and developing a comprehensive assessment system.

Section III: Teaching All Students Successfully - offers explicit guidance in working with students with diverse learning and language needs.

Section IV: Taking Care of Yourself - deals with the issues of balancing personal and professional demands and practical ways for preparing the inevitable substitute.

Section V: Closing the School Year Successfully provides dozens of suggestions that help students continue to learn until the last minute of the school year. It also provides opportunities for the teacher to reflect and plan for more personal enjoyment and professional growth.

In the text you will see a number of shadowed boxes that contain this icon . This hourglass means the box contains one of the following:

- ❖ **Trade Secret:** These items usually deal with district/school policy, procedures and/or school etiquette.

- ❖ **Tip**:   These items are words to the wise and may save you time, energy and/or effort.

- ❖ **Tools**: These refer to forms that will help organize information. Tools also include examples of letters, communiqués, schedules, etc.

- ❖ **Timesavers:** These suggestions help save your precious planning and teaching time.

The editors and authors have also included many pages with this icon in   the lower right-hand corner. This disc symbol means that the page is located on the CD ROM and is available for your immediate use.

# ACKNOWLEDGMENTS

The authors wish to thank the following individuals for giving their time, valuable suggestions, thoughtful critique and consistent support:

| | | | |
|---|---|---|---|
| Nicholas Appleton | Keri Croce | Randa Gick | Shelia Rogers |
| Tiffany Enz-Bodeman | Don Enz | Sandy Glass | Alice Shepard |
| Mary Jo Carpenter | Dawn Enz-Foley | Karen Kimerer | Gloria Smith |
| Barbara Coffman | Donald Freeman | Beth Lang | Photini Spanias |
| | | | Jill Stamm |

A special thank you to:

Monique Davis, program coordinator, for her help in production and editing skills.

Jennifer Showen and Jacquelyn Pritscher for their assistance in production.

Casey Cook for his creative illustrations.

And to our spouses, children (young and grown) and grandchildren for their support.

# ABOUT THE AUTHORS

Authors and Editors:

***Billie Enz*** (Ph.D. Elementary Education) is the Associate Director of the Division of Curriculum and Instruction in the College of Education at Arizona State University. She is responsible for establishing professional development and induction programs with local school districts. Dr. Enz is the author and co-author for several books on new teacher development and mentor training, including: *The Student Teaching Experience: A Developmental Approach, Coaching the Student Teacher: A Developmental Approach, How To Win the Job You Want,* and *Life Cycle of the Career Teacher.* Dr. Enz is a member of the Early Childhood faculty and teaches language and literacy courses. She has co-authored two textbooks in this area, *Teaching Language and Literacy: From Preschool to the Elementary Grades* and *Helping Young Children Learn Language and Literacy: From Birth through Preschool.*

---

***Sharon A. Kortman*** (Ed.D. Curriculum and Instruction) is Lecturer in the College of Education at Arizona State University. She is the Director of Beginning Educator Support Team (BEST), a partnership between university and school districts providing comprehensive support, training, curriculum, courses and resources in the areas of teacher induction, mentoring and preparation for aligning practice to the teaching standards. Dr. Kortman also does consultant work in the areas of personality and interaction styles, which, along with support to the education profession, positively affect student achievement. She is co-author and co-editor of *The BEST Beginning Teacher Experience: Program Facilitator Guide; The BEST Mentoring Experience: Program Facilitator Guide;* accompanying texts for beginning teachers and mentors and *Trade Secrets: Tips, Tools and Timesavers for Middle and Secondary Teachers.*

---

***Connie J. Honaker*** (M.A. English Education) is a Faculty Associate for the Beginning Educator Support Team (BEST) program in the College of Education at Arizona State University. She teaches all levels of BEST courses. She is co-author and co-editor of *The BEST Beginning Teacher Experience: A Framework for Professional Development* and accompanying facilitator guide; *The BEST Mentoring Experience: A Framework for Professional Development* with accompanying facilitator guide; *Trade Secrets: Tips, Tools and Timesavers for Middle and Secondary Teachers*; and Professionals Evolving in their Practice (PEP) and Visitation Coach curriculum. Connie has taught at the elementary and secondary levels and served as an administrator in various roles. Connie is a recipient of the Arizona Distinguished Administrator of the Year Award presented by the Arizona School Administrators Association.

Contributing Authors:

*Barbara Carlile* (Ed.D. Educational Leadership) is a faculty member at Paradise Valley Community College. She has been in the field of education for over twenty years, with interests in staff development, cooperative learning, and second language acquisition. Dr. Carlile is co-author of *Coaching the Student Teacher: A Developmental Approach and The Student Teaching Experience: A Developmental Approach.* Dr. Carlile is author for Chapter 7 – Teaching Language-Minority Students.

*Veronica J. Lyons (Ronnie)* (Ph.D. Instructional Systems) is a consultant for New Directions Institute for Baby's Brain Development. As a teacher and administrator for over 20 years in special education and rehabilitation, her current interests focus on providing appropriate services for students with varied exceptionalities and improving curricular and staff development. Dr. Lyons is co-author for Chapter 6 – Teaching Students with Diverse Abilities.

*Kathleen Rutowski* (Ph.D. Curriculum and Instruction-Special Education) is a lecturer in the Division of Curriculum and Instruction in the College of Education at Arizona State University. Her teaching and research interests lie in the area helping teachers develop inclusive practices and to work collaboratively with special education teachers. Dr. Rutowski is co-author for Chapter 6 – Teaching Students with Diverse Abilities.

Chapter 1

# BEFORE THE STUDENTS ARRIVE

*Putting all the pieces together can be overwhelming.*

Have you ever put together a thousand-piece jigsaw puzzle without a sample of the completed picture? That is how a teacher described his efforts to organize and manage his classroom. The purpose of this book is to provide essential, practical information to help primary, elementary and special educators prepare and successfully negotiate their school year.

**Section A**

# LEARNING ABOUT THE SCHOOL

Congratulations!  You were just hired to teach at Anytown School.  Now you have a thousand things to think about as you prepare for the first day of school.  Knowing how to prepare yourself and your classroom prior to the start of the school year may predict your success as a teacher.  Chapter 1 offers information that will help you:

❖ Understand your professional responsibilities.

❖ Learn about your work environment.

❖ Identify and organize your time, materials and resources.

❖ Design an engaging, efficient classroom.

❖ Develop a personalized lesson planning system.

*"Thousands of things to think about!"*

3

## PROFESSIONALISM

Successful primary and elementary teachers are professionals. They always thoughtfully respond to established policies and consistently implement appropriate classroom procedures. Professionalism also pertains to how the teacher interacts with students, parents, and the school system. The following list offers several aspects of professionalism.

### Students - The teacher:

* Maintains accurate records (attendance and grades) according to school procedure.
* Reviews policies and procedures with students at the beginning of the year and throughout the year as needed.
* Holds all students accountable for following school rules, policies and procedures, such as attendance, homework, and classroom behavior.

### Parents – The teacher:

* Informs parents of policies and procedures, and confirms they have received the information.
* Communicates information about student progress, attendance, and classroom behavior to parents.
* Documents conversations with parents regarding student conferences.

### School System – The teacher:

* Maintains confidentiality regarding student records and school personnel.
* Participates in professional growth opportunities.
* Models appropriate behavior, demeanor, language, dress and humor.
* Maintains strong work ethic, including:
  * Punctuality and adherence to professional workday.
  * Attending department and faculty meetings.
  * Completing paper work in a timely manner.
  * Being prepared to teach and promptly grade assignments.
  * Cooperating with faculty, staff and administration.

 Decisions about your commitment to the profession are made quickly. Remember to sign up for a faculty committee, sponsor a school activity and/or share ideas graciously.

4

**FITTING IN**

Almost all healthy adults have a basic need to belong and gain acceptance in their work environment. To be successful as a teacher, you will need to orient yourself to the physical environment, learn who does what and figure out how to accomplish your instructional goals. You will also need to develop positive professional relationships with administrators, staff and colleagues, and become part of the school community.

However, becoming a part of the school community is not always an easy task. Teachers are inundated with dozens of new names and faces. There never seems to be enough time to learn all the new information and manage all the new responsibilities. The following list provides simple hints to help you fit in with your new colleagues and adjust to your work environment.

### *"Fitting In" Tips*

❖ Eat lunch with other teachers as often as possible. In addition to socializing, it is important to take at least 15-20 minutes to eat, rest a moment, and share ideas and concerns.

❖ Make financial contributions to school collections for wedding or baby shower gifts, hospital flowers, birthday cakes and cards. This monetary token indicates your willingness to become part of a caring, collegial community.

❖ Smile, make positive comments to others, share ideas when asked, and graciously accept ideas when they are offered. These actions allow your colleagues to know that you are open to suggestions, advice and friendship.

❖ Discover who has expertise in specialized areas, such as technology, art and musical talents, and classroom management. Collaborate to share skills and talents.

❖ Be polite to everyone, but avoid frequent contact with negative influences. Sustaining a positive attitude is key to building collegial relationships.

 If you do not have an assigned mentor, look for "friendly faces." These teachers and staff members are almost always willing to help a colleague.

## WHO'S WHO?

Learning who's who and what they do is critical. In addition to remembering names and faces of district/school staff, you should be aware of job descriptions. The following section provides a sample of job titles with spaces for names, phone numbers and email addresses. A brief job description is also included. You will also want the contact information for both the district and the school office. This information may be included in your personalized planning system (see page 33).

### *District Information*

Phone _____ Fax _____ Email_____

Address_____

### *District Office Personnel*

Superintendent_____Phone_____Email_____
This person is the educational leader of the district and is legally responsible for all district personnel and district policies and procedures.

Personnel Director_____Phone_____Email _____
This person is responsible for conducting job searches, interviews and hiring. This person also manages payroll, deductions, and usually helps you enroll for health insurance.

Substitute Clerk_____Phone_____ Email _____
This is the person you call when you need a substitute.

Transportation Director_____ Phone_____ Email _____
This person schedules buses for field trip transportation in addition to managing the district's transportation systems daily.

### *Staff Development Office and Resource Center*

Personnel_____ Phone_____ Email _____

Personnel_____ Phone_____ Email _____
These individuals help teachers expand instructional skills and develop professionally. They also help teachers develop curriculum and can help locate and select appropriate instructional resource materials.

## School Building Information

Phone _____ Fax _____ Email_____

Address_____

## School Building Personnel List

Principal _____ Phone_____ Email _____
This administrator is the educational leader of the school. It is the principal who sets the philosophical direction and work climate of the school site. The principal conducts evaluations of your teaching performance.

Assistant Principal/s _____ Phone_____ Email _____
This person deals directly with student discipline and attendance. Typically the size of the school population determines the number of assistant principals.

Secretary/s _____ Phone_____ Email _____
These staff members are responsible for establishing and maintaining school routines. Secretaries know where things are located and are usually willing to help teachers understand procedures for attendance, field trips and the like.

Clerk/s_____ Phone_____ Email _____
This person supports the secretary in the day-to-day management of the school office. This person can usually show you how to run the copy machine, FAX machine, manage district software, etc.

Nurse/s _____ Phone_____ Email _____
These staff members are responsible for managing the health care records of the students and conduct hearing and vision tests. The nurse maintains immunization records and calls parents if a student is ill.

Building Manager/s_____ Phone_____ Email _____
These employees are responsible for the maintenance of the school site – doing repairs, adjusting desks, and locating classroom furniture.

Counselor/s_____ Phone_____ Email _____
These faculty members manage the student academic schedules and provide support to students and parents in making educational decisions.

Mentor/s _____ Phone_____ Email _____
A mentor will answer day-to-day questions, help you plan and reflect on instructional and management practices and provide support to anything else related to your role as teacher.

## *Grade Level Personnel*

An effective grade level team can achieve results far greater than one individual working alone. It is important to develop a collegial relationship with your team.

Team Leader_____Phone_____Email_____

Team Member_____Phone_____Email_____

Team Member_____Phone_____Email_____

Team Member_____Phone_____Email_____

Team Member_____Phone_____Email_____

## *Special Resource/Assistance Staff*

The titles of these individuals may vary from school to school. They may be called special education resource teachers or English as a Second Language instructors. It is essential to learn these staff members' names, titles and specific responsibilities, as they will contribute to your success in the classroom.

| | Title | Name | Phone | Email |
|---|---|---|---|---|
| Job: | | | | |
| Job: | | | | |
| Job: | | | | |
| Job: | | | | |
| Job: | | | | |

## SCHOOL CALENDAR AND SCHEDULES

Management of time is essential.  The first step in using your time wisely is knowing how much instructional time is available.  Obtain the most up-to-date school calendar from the school secretary.  Note the following dates in your working calendar:

| Activities and Events | Dates | Activities and Events | Dates |
|---|---|---|---|
| * Teacher orientation | _____ | * First day of school | _____ |
| * Grading periods | _____ | * Early release days | _____ |
|  | _____ |  | _____ |
|  | _____ |  | _____ |
|  | _____ |  | _____ |
| * Professional in-service days | _____ | * Parent-teacher conferences | _____ |
|  | _____ |  | _____ |
|  | _____ |  | _____ |
|  | _____ |  | _____ |
| * Last day of school | _____ | * M.L.King Day | _____ |
| * Labor Day | _____ | * Presidents' Day | _____ |
| * Veteran's Day | _____ | * Spring Break | _____ |
| * Thanksgiving | _____ | * Memorial Day | _____ |
| * Winter Break | _____ |  |  |

**The first step in managing your time wisely is
knowing how much instructional time is available.**

9

Likewise, you will also want to know the school's daily schedule. For example, all teachers need to know:

- ❖ When are teachers expected to begin/end the school day?
- ❖ When does instruction begin?
- ❖ When do students arrive?
- ❖ When is lunch served?
- ❖ Are there varying arrival/departure times for different grade levels?
- ❖ When are special schedules implemented?
- ❖ When are the students dismissed?

Elementary teachers need to outline weekly schedules to track special classes, such as library, P.E., computer lab, music and art. As you organize and manage instructional time, know when your class is scheduled to have morning recess and when you are expected to bring your class in from lunch recess.

Using a planning book, design your daily schedule. Be sure to set aside time for daily reflection and preparation.

| | M | T | W | TH | F |
|---|---|---|---|---|---|
| $8^{30}$ | Students Arrive | Students Arrive | Students Arrive | Students Arrive | Students Arrive |
| $9^{00}$ | | | | 9 - $9^{30}$ Art | $9^{30}$ * Linda |
| $10^{00}$ | 10 - $10^{30}$ Music | | | | |
| $11^{00}$ | | | | $11^{00}$ * Erin | |
| $12^{00}$ | Lunch | Lunch | Lunch | Lunch | Lunch |
| $1^{00}$ | | | $1^{00}$ *James | | Students Depart |
| $2^{00}$ | | 2 - $2^{30}$ PE | | 2 - $2^{30}$ PE | Weekly Planning |
| $3^{00}$ | Students Depart | Students Depart | Students Depart | Students Depart | Reflections - Preparation |
| $4^{00}$ | Reflections - Preparation | Reflections – Preparation | Reflections - Preparation | Reflections - Preparation | |
| $4^{45}$ | | | | | |

*Special considerations: Beyond scheduling basics, most elementary teachers have students who require special education or language services where they are "pulled out" of the classroom for support. Design an appropriate schedule to collaborate with colleagues. This will enable you to cooperatively provide instructional assistance for those students in your class. (See examples of weekly planning forms on page 38.)

**POLICIES AND PROCEDURES**

The district/school employee handbook is probably the best source of information about school policies and procedures that are specific to your school. Policies are the rules or guidelines that govern the daily management of the school, while procedures are the specific steps required to accomplish certain policies. For example:

*The school **policy** regarding attendance reads:*

"The teacher is responsible for taking and reporting student attendance accurately at the beginning of each day and after each recess, lunch, special classes, etc. All teachers must record student absences."

*The school attendance **procedures** include:*

1. Take roll in the first 10 minutes of class.

2. Send attendance form to the office immediately.

3. Record attendance in district attendance book (or computer program).

4. Inform students/parents of students' attendance status on report card.

5. Submit monthly information to school secretary on the last day of the month.

 After each break in the school day (recess, lunch, special classes) the teacher should do a head count to confirm all students who began the day are still present; if any student is missing, inform the school secretary immediately.

You are held accountable for knowing and upholding the school's policies and procedures regarding students, instructions, activities and administrative concerns.

**Student Concerns:**

How do I...

- ❖ Grade and report student progress?_____
- ❖ Secure health care for students?_____
- ❖ Access student information?_____
- ❖ Make student referrals?_____
- ❖ Assign homework?_____
- ❖ Respond to emergency situations, such as a fire, tornado, earthquake or bomb threat? _____

**Instructional Needs:**

How do I...

- ❖ Check out audio-visual equipment?_____
- ❖ Collaborate with special education staff?_____
- ❖ Collaborate with second language staff?_____
- ❖ Schedule and conduct field trips?_____
- ❖ Order trade books?_____
- ❖ Order resources, materials and supplies?_____

**Administrative Issues:**

How do I...

- ❖ Complete and report attendance/tardies?_____
- ❖ Manage lunch tickets/lunch money?_____
- ❖ Secure a substitute?_____
- ❖ Reinforce a school-wide discipline plan?_____
- ❖ Raise funds?_____

12

## RESOURCES, MATERIALS AND SUPPLIES

New teachers often walk into empty rooms. If this is the case, you will need to begin the process of ordering or locating supplies immediately. This inventory will help you know what you need to order. See school secretary for guidance in ordering supplies or reporting broken furniture and equipment.

### *Classroom Checklist*

| *Classroom Furniture Equipment* | *Classroom Materials* |
|---|---|
| ____ Teacher desk and chair | ____ Student texts |
| ____ Tables | ____ Teacher's editions |
| ____ File cabinet | ____ Maps |
| ____ Storage cabinet | ____ Globe |
| ____ Computer | ____ Subject equipment |
| ____ Student desks & chairs | ____ Subject materials |
| ____ Classroom TV Monitor | |

| *Filing Cabinet* | *Storage Cabinet* |
|---|---|
| ____ Hanging folders | ____ Chalk and erasers |
| ____ Manila file folders | ____ White board markers/eraser |
| ____ Index tabs | ____ Paper cutter |
| | ____ Bulletin board supplies |

| *Audio-Visual Equipment* | |
|---|---|
| ____ Overhead projector | ____ Computer/software |
| ____ Tape-player/recorder | ____ Earphone set |
| ____ Video-player | ____ Adaptive devices |
| ____ Extension cord | ____ Plug adapter |

| *For the Desk* | |
|---|---|
| ____ Scissors | ____ Thank you notes and cards |
| ____ Stapler, staples, staple remover | ____ Postage stamps |
| ____ Scotch tape and masking tape | ____ School forms: |
| ____ Pens, pencils, markers | ____attendance |
| ____ Paper clips (small and large) | ____nurse's referral |
| ____ Post-Its, note pads, note paper | ____hall passes |
| ____ Dictionary | ____ Single and three-hole punch |
| ____ Ruler | ____ Straight pins and tacks |
| ____ Assorted tools - hammer, pliers | ____ Ziploc bags (assorted sizes) |
| ____ Glue, glue stick, rubber cement | ____ Safety pins - all sizes |

 It is important to test each piece of equipment and check the safety of tables or chairs. Use this checklist as a way to track each item that needs repair.

## *Additional Checklist for Primary Classrooms*

| *Math Manipulatives* | *Science Equipment* |
|---|---|
| _____ Flannel boards and felt pieces | _____ Cage/Aquarium for class pets |
| _____ Rulers and tape measures | _____ Prisms |
| _____ Measuring cups and spoons | _____ Eye dropper |
| _____ Clocks | _____ Compasses |
| _____ Number lines | _____ Telescope |
| _____ Age-appropriate math game | _____ Batteries/copper wire |
| _____ Thermometers | _____ Rock sets |
| _____ Meter/yard stick | _____ Planting trays |
| _____ Graph paper | _____ Rock/fossil/insect collections |
| _____ Pattern cubes | _____ Magnets/iron filings |
| _____ Beads | _____ Cooking equipment |
| _____ Weights, balance, scales | _____ Microscope/Magnifying glasses |
| _____ Play coins & money | |

| *Reading/Language Arts* | *Social Studies* |
|---|---|
| _____ Alphabet/Handwriting chart | _____ Globes |
| _____ Big books (K-3) | _____ U.S. and world maps |
| _____ Pocket charts (K-3) | _____ City and road maps |
| _____ Dozens of paperback books | _____ Travel posters |
| _____ Chart paper | _____ Community worker sets |
| _____ Writing paper | _____ Presidents' photographs |
| _____ Pens, pencils, markers | _____ Timelines |

| *Music* | *Art* |
|---|---|
| _____ Tapes/CDs | _____ Markers and crayons |
| _____ Listening earphones | _____ Yarn |
| _____ Tape/CD player | _____ Tempera paints and brushes |
| _____ Autoharp | _____ Watercolor sets |
| _____ Bells | _____ Easels |
| _____ Percussion sticks | _____ Smocks |
| _____ Flute-a-phone | _____ Construction paper |
| _____ Drum | _____ Clay |

| *Physical Education* | *Dramatic Play* |
|---|---|
| _____ Balls of all types | _____ Prop boxes |
| _____ Jump ropes | _____ Puppets |
| _____ Hula hoops | _____ Playhouse props |

| *Cleaning Materials* | *Health Kit* |
|---|---|
| _____ Cleaners/detergent | _____ Band-Aids/tissues |
| _____ Rags/sponges/paper towels | _____ Antibiotic gel |

In addition to basic classroom supplies, you need to know how to locate specific instructional resources that are available through the district. Most districts have a media or curriculum center that is a repository for materials that are shared across schools. The district media/curriculum center usually offers a range of instructional videotapes, computer software, CD-ROM discs and audiocassettes for every subject that is taught. Ask district staff development personnel for a brief tour of this facility. You will also want to learn how to check out instructional materials and equipment, and inquire about the length of time materials can be loaned.

After you have reviewed the district's resources, consider other sources of material, such as discount teacher supply companies that will send catalogs of their merchandise. For example:

Creative Educational Surplus
9801 James Circle
Bloomington, MN 55431

Likewise, you may wish to review books that identify reasonable resources for teachers; for instance,

"Free and Almost Free Things for Teachers,"
by Susan Osborn,
published by Putnam Publishing Group.

### The Joys of Junk

Teachers soon discover that many of their colleagues frequent garage sales, thrift stores and even junkyards in their quest for teaching resources! Experienced teachers regularly find wonderful, interesting and inexpensive supplies, resources, and classroom furniture and equipment at these places.

**"This will make a great lab tray!"**

Another resource for teachers is the Internet. Following is a list of Websites that offer a wide range of instructional materials that you may browse through from the comfort of a home computer.

*The Internet is an exciting option for instructional resources.*

### *Websites*

*http://www.yahoo.com/Education/K_12/*
Yahoo site for K-12 education resources. Yahoo is one of the major search engines for the World Wide Web which, will take searchers to a wealth of educational materials and resources.

*http://www.yahoo.com/Recreation/Travel/Virtual_Field_Trips/*
Links to virtual field trips of K-12 interest. Many are interactive and include lesson plans.

*http://www.yahoo.com/Education/K_12/Teaching/Lesson_Plans/*
Links to lesson plans in all content areas of K-12 interest.

*http://www.col-ed.org/cur/*
From the Columbia Education Center. Lesson plans organized by topic (science, math, language arts, social studies, miscellaneous) and grade levels K-12.

*http://www.col-ed.org/smcnws/msres/curriculum.html*
Internet-based lesson plans and resources for teachers and students.

*http://www.clarityconnect.com/webpages/terri/sites.html*
Great sites for math teachers.

*http://www.teachnet.com/manage.html*
Classroom management ideas. Mostly elementary; some middle and high school ideas.

*http://www.teachnet.com/*
Variety of tools for teachers K-12, including projects, discussion groups, tips for classroom decor, organization & time management, lesson plans, classroom p.r. and humor.

*http://www.ceismc.gatech.edu/BusyT/*
The Busy Teacher Website. Teacher resources and ideas, projects by curriculum area for secondary teachers, separate elementary section. Links to quality educational Websites. Winner of Top 5% Website Award.

*gopher://ericir.syr.edu:70/11/Lesson/Newton_Apple/Lesson_Plan*
Lesson Plans from ERIC.

*www.ed.gov*
For access to the U.S. Department of Education homepage to access current information in education and to access ED-funded internet resources.

*www.middleweb.com*
Offers help to new teachers to teach in middle school.

*www.ericir.cvr.edu/virtual/lessons*
Provides information on specific curriculum areas.

*www.kdp.org*
Offers a wealth of insights on topics of interest to the first-year teacher.

*www.doubletakermagazine.org/teacherguide*
Offers thematic units of study on race relations, work, sense of place, beyond political ideology, and sense of identity.

*www.webteacher.org*
Offers additional resource for high school teachers.

*www.eagle.com/teacher*
Helps teachers utilize newspaper editorial cartoons as teaching tools.

*www.education.usatoday.com*
Offers interactive projects and global education resources for educators, students and parents.

*www.whitehouse.gov/sh/welcome.htm*
Posts the newsletter, The Whitehouse for Kids, which includes current information about government and the happenings of the White House.

*www.edweek.org*
Accesses online magazines and timely topics, features stories, current events, research, news briefs, and comments by renowned educators.

*www.pacific.net/~mandel*
Provides basic teaching tips to inexperienced teachers at all levels, K-12.

*www.foothil.net~moorek/index.html*
For specific advice, help, and direction on a variety of topics, such as classroom management, lesson design, checking for understanding, and checking student work.

*www.geocities.com*
Will lead to a variety of topics.

*www.chainreaction.asu.edu*
Online magazine for middle-school science teachers.

*www.ascd.org*
Online newsletter and leads to other Websites on specific topics.

*http://lcweb.loc.gov*
Accesses information from the Library of Congress.

*www.books4educ.com*
Online bookstore.

*www.amazon.com*
Online bookstore that provides reviews of music, videos and books.

*www.teachnet.com*
Provides lesson ideas and other resources.

*www.iloveteaching.com*
Provides information and tips on a variety of topics, such as management and discipline.

(See Chapter 6 for Websites of special education professional organizations, which also offer information on resources.)

While most teachers find an empty classroom with no supplies, others inherit a room from a teacher who has left everything to the next occupant. In this case, it is important to conduct a thorough inventory by using the checklists on pages 13 and 14.

 As you survey your supplies, to clean equipment and reorganize material, develop a "Where Did I Put This?" list to help you quickly locate materials you do not use on an everyday basis.

 Invest in several plastic containers, about 15 to 20 gallons in size, with snap tight lids.

While cardboard boxes are inexpensive, they break apart rather quickly and cannot withstand basement floods, insects or mice as well as plastic boxes. Be sure to mark the contents of the box on a piece of construction paper and place it inside the see-through box so that you can easily see what types of materials/resources this box contains.

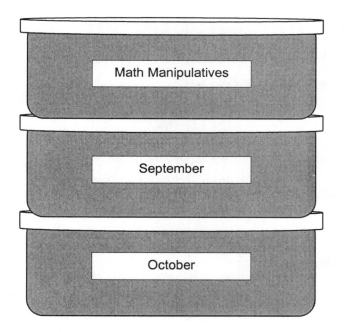

**These plastic containers are stackable, which makes storage even easier.**

## WELCOME TO THE COMMUNITY

Becoming acquainted with your community is essential to your success as a teacher. It is important for you to feel comfortable in your environment. If you are new to your community, you may have many questions about the area. Some common concerns to consider include:

**Commuting** - Learn your schedules and the flow of "commuting" traffic. Drive a few trial runs to school during the times when you would normally commute. For example, if you plan to drive to school each morning, drive it at least once during the time you would normally commute to school to find the best route, and to check traffic patterns and time. The same can be said if you plan to use subways, trains and buses.

**News** - Subscribe to a local newspaper. Suburban and local newspapers generally carry more school and local news than large city newspapers and help the teacher become attuned to local attitudes, concerns, ideas and values.

Other areas to check for new-to-the-community teachers may include:

- ❑ Housing
- ❑ Emergency phone numbers
- ❑ Medical facilities
- ❑ Child care
- ❑ Grocery store, pharmacy, bookstores, shopping malls
- ❑ Post office location and zip code
- ❑ Utility companies that serve your area
- ❑ Recreation, exercise, sports activities and parks
- ❑ Public library
- ❑ College or university
- ❑ Radio and television stations
- ❑ Banking institutions
- ❑ Religious institutions

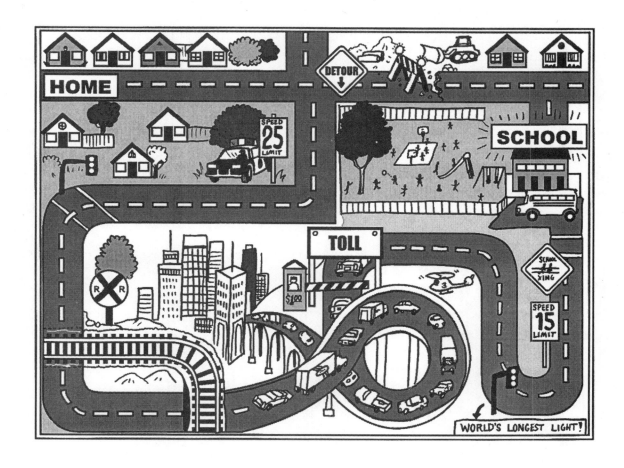

**Planning the best time for commuting to and from work
will maximize your work hours.**

**Notes:**

**Section B**

## ORGANIZING THE LEARNING ENVIRONMENT

The classroom environment you create reflects your teaching style and beliefs about teaching. The way you organize desks and display work will make students feel welcome and encourage them to learn. This section provides specific suggestions to consider as you prepare your classroom to be an organized, efficient, attractive place for working and learning. The section offers ideas for teachers who must share class space with other colleagues.

*"Let's begin!"*

## DESIGNING YOUR CLASSROOM

Not all classrooms are created equal. Some rooms are perfectly square, while others feel more like a wedge of pie. Some rooms are large with a high ceiling and skylights, and some are small and dark. Some rooms have built-in storage cabinets, shelves and closets, while other rooms may only be endowed with four walls! The first rule of classroom design is "work with the space you are given." You can't change the fact that your room is tiny, but you can maximize the space you have by thoughtful planning. Begin by drawing a floor plan (to scale) of the classroom you have been assigned. Be sure to identify where the doors and windows are located, and label any unique features, such as a sink, bathroom or closet. Next, look for electric outlets (you can mark them by placing an "x" on the floor diagram), then identify where the chalkboard, bulletin boards and/or television monitor are stationed.

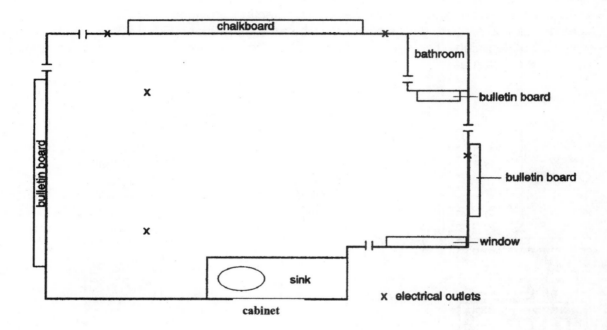

**Primary Floor Plan**

### *Classroom Considerations*

In addition to the general information about classroom design, elementary teachers usually need to consider a number of other factors, including:

**Flexibility -** Can desks be moved easily if you need more space to play inside games, practice a dance or conduct a science experiment?

**Functional Logic -** Elementary teachers need to make sure centers are well placed and support learning easily. This occurs when teachers logically consider the functions of the centers they are using and where these centers need to be placed in order to best support children's learning and make good use of classroom space. For instance:

- ❖ Are all potentially messy areas, such as a cooking or art center, near the sink where cleanup can be easily managed?

- ❖ Are quiet areas, such as library and writing centers, placed away from potentially noisier areas, such as the block or the dramatic play center?

- ❖ Is the science center close to sunlight (or bright artificial light) so that you could germinate seeds and easily sustain plant life?

- ❖ Is the listening center and computer center close to electrical outlets?

- ❖ Are all areas accessible to students who have special needs?

 Plan areas for student belongings. Provide a space for backpacks, lunch boxes, umbrellas, jackets, show-and-tell items and lost-and-found.

## ROOM ARRANGEMENTS: MORE THAN DESKS

After you have drawn your classroom floor plan, consider arrangement of furniture and equipment. Veteran teachers suggest you make several copies of the floor plan and experiment with furniture arrangement on paper before you begin to move real (and heavy) desks and tables.

You will probably experiment with a variety of classroom arrangements. However you decide to arrange students, you will need to consider:

**Sight** - Students' attention is sustained longer when they can clearly see the teacher and frequently used instructional areas.

   ❖   Can all students see the chalkboard or TV monitor easily?
   ❖   Are students with visual or other impairments seated appropriately?

**Traffic Flow** - Cluttered classrooms are distracting and can become dangerous. Keep access to storage/supply areas and exits clear.

   ❖   Are the aisles between desks and tables wide enough so that you and the students can move easily from one part of the room to another?
   ❖   Are the aisles and doorways easily accessible for students who are physically challenged?

**Accessibility** - Teachers who can view the whole classroom at a glance and quickly move about the classroom have greater control of student behavior and thus maximize learning.

   ❖   Can you move through the classroom easily and quickly?
   ❖   Can you see all students in the room?

**Instructional Match** - Your organization of students' desks usually reflects your beliefs about instruction and how students learn.

   ❖   Does the seating arrangement support your instructional practices?
   ❖   Does the seating arrangement facilitate student learning?

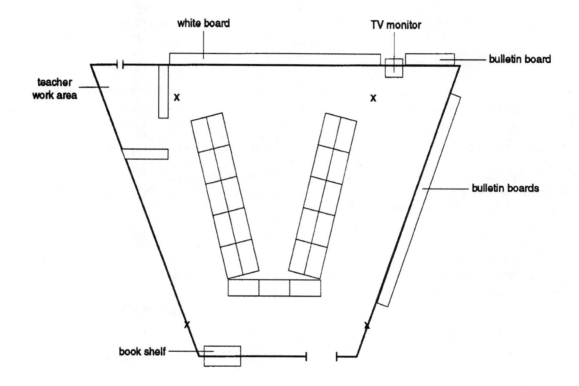

white board

TV monitor

bulletin board

teacher work area

x          x

bulletin boards

book shelf

**Elementary Floor Plan**

# WALL SPACE AND BULLETIN BOARDS

The way you utilize wall space and the types of bulletin boards you create send a powerful message about the tone of your classroom. Blank walls are boring and may transmit a cold feeling, while bright colors and interesting, purposeful displays engage your students.

Some schools have specific, framed corkboards for you to use for displays. Some schools have tack-able walls where almost all wall space can be used to exhibit student work. Teachers may feel overwhelmed when they begin to plan bulletin boards. Remember, you do not have to have every bit of wall space decorated before school starts. In fact, you will want to provide adequate wall space for your students to share their school work and artistic creations.

Design functional bulletin boards that share specific information, remind students about classroom expectations and/or motivate student learning. For example:

### All Year

Student Birthdays
Calendar
Weekly Assignment Calendar
Students' Work
Progress Charts
Class/School Schedule
Student Self-Portraits
   (See page 29.)

### Seasonal/Special Events

Seasons
Beginning/closing of year
Open House
Holidays

### Instructional

Curriculum Charts
Current Events - local campus,
   local community, state, national and
   international
Instructional Unit Display
Weather Charts
Compass Direction Chart

### Functional Bulletin Boards

Discipline Plan
Classroom Helpers Chart
Center Rotation Chart
Lunch Count/Attendance Chart
   (See page 29.)

### Teacher Work Space Bulletin Board

Teachers often have a small bulletin board by their desk that displays:
Emergency Information
Alternative School Schedules
Menus
Duty Schedules
Language Experience Stories

 Use bright-colored material (in school colors) to cover bulletin boards. Fabric lasts longer than paper, is slow to fade, and does not show pin, tack or staple holes.

**Self-Portraits -** Many teachers begin the year by taking pictures of their students on the first day of school. They use a digital camera and process them on the computer or develop at a one-hour photo lab so the pictures are ready by the second day of school. Students are then given their photo and an 8" X 11" piece of construction paper. As homework, students are assigned to decorate this paper with their picture and name, and then draw something special about themselves, e.g., skills, talents, friends or family. The students bring the artwork back the following day. Then over the next few days, during the last 15 - 20 minutes of class, the students describe their "self-portrait." This artwork is then displayed. Students and teachers enjoy getting to know each other. In addition, the pictures help make the classroom a warm learning environment.

**Attendance/Lunch Count Chart -** As the students enter the room, they routinely take their attendance and signal their choice for lunch by placing a different colored and labeled Popsicle stick in their name pocket located on the attendance chart. For example, a white stick means the child has brought lunch and will only need to purchase milk. A striped stick means the child will purchase a hot meal and the dotted stick means the child will purchase a salad bar lunch. If a lunch stick is not in the name pocket, it means the child is absent. The attendance helper simply counts the different types of sticks and completes the lunch form while the teacher completes the attendance slip.

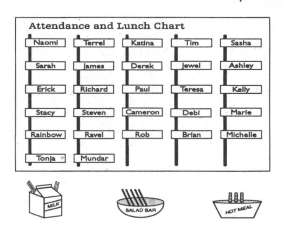

## SHARING A ROOM WITH YOUR COLLEAGUE

Some teachers do not have a room to call their own. Often these teachers travel from one classroom to another. Initially, room changing can be disorienting. If you are a traveling teacher consider:

**Carry Your Office with You -** Traveling teachers have found that using a small (19" to 21"), wheeled suitcase with a retractable handle offers many advantages. These teachers easily transport their instructional materials to class and are also able to keep the students' homework papers organized and close at hand. Some teachers keep desk supplies in their rolling desk.

*"Have bag -- will teach."*

**Art-on-a-Cart -** In many elementary schools, art, music, P.E. and resource teachers are also travelers. In these cases the equipment may be too large for a suitcase. These teachers suggest using a grocery-store shopping cart (or some version of this convenience) to be an adequate "roving classroom." In many cases, these teachers have a place in each classroom where they store the students' projects. This prevents the children's work (e.g., clay pots) from being lost or damaged.

**Sharing a Room -** In some schools, teachers share classrooms. In this case it is customary to share wall and planning space. In most cases, both teachers have their own file cabinet, desk or table. Communication, patience, flexibility, trust and a good sense of humor help manage this situation. If you are in this scenario, be sure to:

❖ Return furniture to its original arrangement.

❖ Take a minute or two to clean up floor, desks and tables.

❖ Return all supplies/materials to original drawers and shelves.

❖ Respect the other teacher's desk and personal belongings.

*"Is that my stapler?"*

**Job Sharing -** This is a unique personnel arrangement where two teachers share one teaching position; for instance, two teachers share one class of primary children. In most cases, the teachers involved have worked together as teammates or colleagues and both feel comfortable with sharing students and a classroom. This situation may occur when two teachers request to work part-time. These teachers meet regularly and have well-established communication patterns that assist in their shared responsibilities.

**Notes:**

## Section C

## DESIGNING A PERSONALIZED PLANNING SYSTEM

Your lesson plan book is one of the main keys to organizing and managing your time and the curriculum. Many teachers find the standard commercial lesson plan book difficult to use; it is hard to write all of your thoughts in the small boxes typically provided. One suggestion that can be helpful is to develop an individualized planning system, a teaching organizer!

This section provides models and samples of planning schemata and suggestions that might help you organize critical information. Begin by purchasing a large three-ring binder. Copy any of the forms illustrated in this section you believe to be useful. You may modify these forms or create new forms that are appropriate for your needs. Finally, organize the sections in your planning book for flexibility in adapting to daily teaching needs.

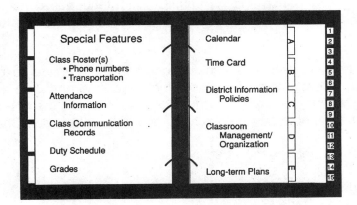

 An effective way to organize your calendar, schedules and additional information quickly is to create an A to Z section in your notebook. File the calendar under "C" and the schedule under "S." Label each inclusion in the upper right-hand corner for easy retrieval.

*Possible Contents:*

**Class Record/s -** These include students' names, phone numbers, addresses, and special notes about the students; for example, parents' surname (if different from the student's) and/or information about a student's physical needs. The class record may also be used to organize a student code system that helps alphabetize materials (see page 44 for student code system).

**Calendar -** Keeping track of both immediate (daily/weekly) and long-range (monthly/yearly) deadlines is essential for effective teachers. Use a school calendar or transfer dates to your own working calendar. Many schools also publish weekly updates that are invaluable for keeping up with committee meetings and paperwork deadlines.

**Long-term Plan -** A year-long curriculum overview maximizes content integration, supports your efforts to order resources/supplemental materials and allows you to make the most effective use of instructional time. To begin, work with your department chair, mentor teacher or grade-level team and review the district curriculum guide for scope and sequence (see page 35).

**Weekly/Daily Plans -** A week-long outline/overview for the instructional events that will occur in the classroom includes a timeframe with "skeletal" daily plans. Be sure to consult or collaborate with special education teachers or personnel supporting students in your classroom (see pages 38-41).

**Student Attendance Records -** Keeping your attendance log close at hand is essential for accurately tracking attendance and communicating attendance concerns to parents and school administrators. All teachers are required to monitor student attendance (see pages 46-48).

**Parental Contact Log -** All teachers should document calls made to parents. The contact log should provide specific information about the time and date of the call, the name of the parent/guardian you spoke to, the reason for the call, the parental response to the concern, and, finally, note any actions that need to be taken (see Chapter 4).

**Special Features -** The notebook may also include:
- ❖ Seating chart/s
- ❖ Duty schedule
- ❖ Transportation guide (See page 49)
- ❖ Birthday chart (See page 50)
- ❖ Substitute plans (See Chapter 9)
- ❖ Student grades (See Chapter 5)

## THE LONG-TERM PLANNING REALITIES

To begin "to get the whole picture," a new teacher should plan a tentative year-long topical overview. Knowing what lies ahead gives you an opportunity to see how you can make all the curricular pieces fit together, smoothly! To begin this process, consult the district curriculum guide and discuss plans with your grade-level leader, mentor or a veteran teacher who teaches the same content.

| Subject/s | Math | | |
|---|---|---|---|
| *September* | 1. Numeration<br>2. Review addition/ subtraction facts<br>3. Time<br>4. Less than/ Greater than | | |
| *October* | | | |
| *November* | | | |
| *December* | | | |
| *January* | | | |
| *February* | | | |
| *March* | | | |
| *April* | | | |
| *May* | | | |

## THEMATIC UNITS

Thematic instruction is an exciting way to help students learn. The following special feature describes how Mrs. Lopez, a middle school teacher, begins to develop an integrated, thematic unit on the Way West. She identifies the interests of her students and works with district and state curriculum guidelines to develop her unit.

### KWL Chart

To determine topics of interest, Mrs. Lopez uses the KWL strategy. The KWL chart below presents the initial outcome of these efforts. KWL stands for "What We **K**now, What We **W**ant to Learn, and What We **L**earned." Prior to the unit students complete the Know and Want columns.

"The Way West Instructional Unit"

| What We Know About | What We Want To Learn | What We Learned |
|---|---|---|
| ❖ Gold Rush in 1849<br><br>❖ Wagon trains<br><br>❖ Free land<br><br>❖ Many people died | ❖ Who were the people that left their homes?<br><br>❖ How long did wagon trips take?<br><br>❖ Why did the Indians attack the wagon trains?<br><br>❖ How did the people survive this trip? | ❖ Irish people were one of the largest groups because of the Potato Famine.<br><br>❖ The people survived the trip because their families were strong, they planned well and they rationed their food. |

Utilizing the information attained, Mrs. Lopez developed a curriculum plan. This process allowed her to consider district and state requirements and merge them with the students' interests and prior knowledge.

 At the end of the instructional time ask students to summarize what they have learned. Have students record in the "What We Learned" column on their KWL chart.

## CURRICULUM INTEGRATION

A topic web is used as a planning strategy to:

- ❖ See natural linkages between topics in the curriculum.
- ❖ Consider the range of resources that could be used.
- ❖ Develop a tentative timeline.

### *Topic Web*

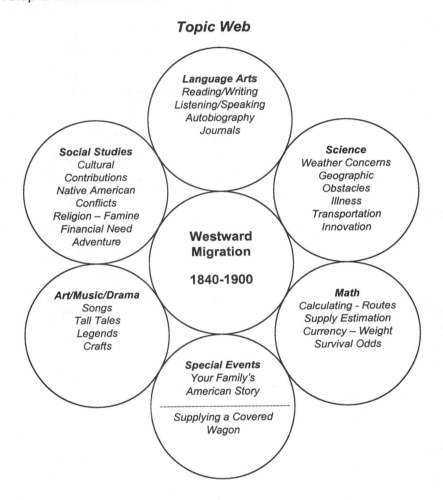

### *Sample Lesson Plan Form*

| Subject | Topics | Objectives | Activities |
|---|---|---|---|
| Social Studies | Cultural Contributions | To identify the cultural contributions of the Irish community | Learn Irish ballads<br><br>Analyze text of ballads for contributions |

## WEEKLY OVERVIEW                           Week of: _____

Weekly plans help you transition from the monthly long-term plan to daily plans. The week-at-a-glance provides a guide for development of daily detailed lesson plans.

|  | Monday | Tuesday | Wednesday | Thursday | Friday |
|---|---|---|---|---|---|
| Before School |  |  |  |  |  |
| AM |  |  |  |  |  |
|  |  |  |  |  |  |
|  |  |  |  |  |  |
| Lunch |  |  |  |  |  |
| PM |  |  |  |  |  |
|  |  |  |  |  |  |
|  |  |  |  |  |  |
| After school |  |  |  |  |  |

The weekly overview helps you see the week at a glance.

**Sustained Silent Planning Time -** It is often more productive to develop your lesson plans in the classroom since all your materials and resources are close at hand. Therefore, you should plan to stay at school at least one day a week until your planning is completed or consider the following tip.

 Frequently, teachers' days are extremely tiring, both physically and mentally. Therefore, experienced teachers recommend that you arrange some planning time on the weekend, if necessary, rather than staying late at school each day.

 Consider using a software program designed for teachers. These generally include several formats for weekly and daily lesson plans. Find a form that suits your unique needs.

Most beginning teachers report feeling rushed for time and often cut short planning time. Successful teachers *focus on lesson planning*. Good lessons promote interesting lessons, which, in turn, foster better classroom behavior.

# DAILY LESSON PLANNING

## *Lesson Plan Development*

Developing lesson plans is developing answers to four questions:

1. What do you want the students to know or do?

2. What resources/materials will you use to teach this information?

3. What instructional techniques will you use to teach these concepts?

4. How will you assess the students' level of understanding?

Your lesson plan book serves as an outline/overview for the instructional events that will occur in your classroom. An actual "lesson plan" needs to be more fully developed as you begin your teaching career so you have a clear blueprint for instruction (see page 41).

**Learner Outcomes:**
- What do you want the students to know or do?

**Introduction:**
- How will you connect students' prior knowledge to new learning?
- How will you motivate students' interest and learning?

**Instructional Input:**
- In what ways will students be actively involved in the lesson?
- What techniques or strategies will you use to teach this concept?
- What content needs to be taught?
- How will you logically sequence presentation of this content?

**Evaluation:**
- How will you determine/document students' level of understanding?
- How will students' comprehension influence subsequent lessons?

**Closure:**
- How will you help students retain or apply information they learned?

**Resources:**
- What resources/materials will you use to teach this information?
- What preparations do you need to do before the lesson is taught?

**Differentiation:**
- How will you adapt lessons to accommodate all learners?

*The First Day*

## Sample Lesson Plan Form

| | | |
|---|---|---|
| Subject: | Class/Period: | Date: |

**LEARNER OUTCOMES:** Lesson objective and sub-objectives

State Standard:            District Outcome:

**INTRODUCTION:** Focus, anticipatory set, motivation

**INSTRUCTIONAL INPUT:** Teaching procedures and student activities / Adaptions for students with special needs

**EVALUATION:** Checking for understanding and lesson assessment

**CLOSURE:** Lesson summation of learners new knowledge

**ASSIGNMENTS:** Independent practice and homework

**RESOURCES:** Equipment, materials, teaching aids

## TIME FOR REFLECTION

Time is one of a teacher's most valuable commodities. To make the best use of your time, set aside 10-15 minutes at the end of each day for reflection. Think about all of the events that went well and why; then think about what you would change about the day to enhance student learning. These ideas and insights build thoughtful teaching practice.

 It often helps to use your lesson plan to guide your reflection.

❖ Use a colored pen to jot in the margins of the lesson plan.

❖ Did a lesson run longer or shorter than you expected? Why?

❖ Did you get a "brain storm" in the middle of instruction?

❖ Did you capitalize on a "teachable" moment?

Jot down the idea to help you remember it again. Try using the Lesson Reflection Form included on the next page. It can then be filed with the lesson plan.

***Taking time to reflect is important for growth.***

 Time for reflection about the lesson will not be complete until you review students' responses to the lesson.

42

**FORMS**

## *Curriculum Lesson Reflection Form*

Date _____Subject _____Grade _____Hour _____

## To Celebrate!! (Identify one positive element to include next time.)

## To Grow On!! (Identify one element to improve next time.)

## To Implement!! (How will you implement area to improve?)

## Student Codes: A Management Idea

 Student code numbers help organize students, grouping and paperwork at all instructional levels.

*Set Up:*

1. Alphabetize your class by last names.
2. Number your students on your alphabetized class roster.
3. The numbers you assign become the students' code numbers for the year.
4. Assign each student his/her code number and require it to be in the upper right-hand corner of all work. For example: Allan Adams #1, Alice Bonet #2.

*Uses:*

**Missing Work** - Before checking papers, quickly put them in numerical order (or have a student do it). Glance through papers -- missing numbers equal missing work.

**Filing/Recording Grades** - It takes only moments to record and file alphabetized assignments.

**Keeping Track of Books and Materials** - Number all class sets of books and/or class tools, such as rulers, scissors and computers. When distributing/assigning such items, match numbers to code numbers. This ends the old "Somebody took my book" lament! Finally, when it is time to collect these materials, any losses will be attributed to the responsible students.

**Grouping** (for any activity) - The teacher is able to group students very quickly; for example, odd numbers make one team, even numbers the other, or numbers 1 through 6 may go to the LRC.

**Random Grouping, Assignments, Rotations** - The teacher keeps a container holding numbered discs or papers. When needed, draw a number/s out, lottery style. This can be used to give a random order for presenting reports and/or forming groups.

The following pages offer several samples of forms to help organize your personalized planning system.

## Class Record

| Student Name | Address | Phone/Email | Notes* |
|---|---|---|---|
| 1. | | | |
| 2. | | | |
| 3. | | | |
| 4. | | | |
| 5. | | | |
| 6. | | | |
| 7. | | | |
| 8. | | | |
| 9. | | | |
| 10. | | | |
| 11. | | | |
| 12. | | | |
| 13. | | | |
| 14. | | | |
| 15. | | | |
| 16. | | | |
| 17. | | | |
| 18. | | | |
| 19. | | | |
| 20. | | | |
| 21. | | | |
| 22. | | | |
| 23. | | | |
| 24. | | | |
| 25. | | | |
| 26. | | | |
| 27. | | | |
| 28. | | | |

*Guardian's or Parents' last name.

# Student Attendance Chart

Month: _____

Dates:

| Names | M | T | W | Th | F | M | T | W | Th | F | M | T | W | Th | F | M | T | W | Th | F |
|---|---|---|---|---|---|---|---|---|---|---|---|---|---|---|---|---|---|---|---|---|
| 1. | | | | | | | | | | | | | | | | | | | | |
| 2. | | | | | | | | | | | | | | | | | | | | |
| 3. | | | | | | | | | | | | | | | | | | | | |
| 4. | | | | | | | | | | | | | | | | | | | | |
| 5. | | | | | | | | | | | | | | | | | | | | |
| 6. | | | | | | | | | | | | | | | | | | | | |
| 7. | | | | | | | | | | | | | | | | | | | | |
| 8. | | | | | | | | | | | | | | | | | | | | |
| 9. | | | | | | | | | | | | | | | | | | | | |
| 10. | | | | | | | | | | | | | | | | | | | | |
| 11. | | | | | | | | | | | | | | | | | | | | |
| 12. | | | | | | | | | | | | | | | | | | | | |
| 13. | | | | | | | | | | | | | | | | | | | | |
| 14. | | | | | | | | | | | | | | | | | | | | |
| 15. | | | | | | | | | | | | | | | | | | | | |
| 16. | | | | | | | | | | | | | | | | | | | | |
| 17. | | | | | | | | | | | | | | | | | | | | |
| 18. | | | | | | | | | | | | | | | | | | | | |
| 19. | | | | | | | | | | | | | | | | | | | | |
| 20. | | | | | | | | | | | | | | | | | | | | |
| 21. | | | | | | | | | | | | | | | | | | | | |
| 22. | | | | | | | | | | | | | | | | | | | | |
| 23. | | | | | | | | | | | | | | | | | | | | |
| 24. | | | | | | | | | | | | | | | | | | | | |
| 25. | | | | | | | | | | | | | | | | | | | | |
| 26. | | | | | | | | | | | | | | | | | | | | |

The year can be started on a supplemental attendance sheet until permanent rosters are printed and made available. Attendance in your district may be recorded on computer. Attendance records are required by the state for funding purposes so be sure to know your responsibilities for recording and reporting. Attendance policies are often governed by state legislation and are usually quite similar across districts.

### *Record Keeping*

**Record Keeping:** Example of record-keeping symbols. Be sure to know **your** system.

Absence

Excused Absence

Unexcused Absence

Tardy

Excused Tardy

Unexcused Tardy

Field trip, school activity, nurse's office

Suspension

Late entry (draw line *to date of entry*)

Withdraw (draw line *to end of semester*)

If a student is missing school, immediately contact the parents. The following page offers an example of a letter regarding attendance.

**Attendance Problem Letter to Parents**

The following is a sample letter that is usually generated with the cooperation of the administrative office.

 GREEN VALLEY HILLS ELEMENTARY SCHOOL

February 27

Dear Mrs. Jones,

We have noted a high number of absences and tardies for Martin. Martin has a total of <u>twenty-two</u> absences and <u>twenty-one</u> tardies since the start of school in August. He has accumulated <u>twelve</u> more absences since our last letter to you in December. We are required to let you know once your child has reached ten absences, ten tardies or both. We are committed to a high quality learning experience and absences and tardies can impact your child's learning potential.

The bell rings at 7:40 a.m. and arrival after 7:45 a.m. is considered tardy. Please remind Martin and whoever drops Martin off of the importance of arriving to school on time and to try to be here before 7:45 a.m. We are also required to inform our District Attendance Officer whenever a child has 10 or more absences or tardies. If you have any questions or concerns, please feel free to call us at anytime. Thank you so much for your participation in the education of your child.

Sincerely,

*Kim Phifer*

Kim Phifer
Principal

*Shauna Wilbraham*

Shauna Wilbraham
Attendance Clerk

 At the elementary school level excessive student absences are usually an indication that the parents are in need of guidance and support.
In these cases the school's social worker should be consulted.

## Transportation Chart

**Bus Riders**

**Walkers**

_____

_____

_____

_____

_____

_____

_____

_____

**Day Care Van**

**After School Care**

_____

_____

_____

_____

_____

_____

_____

_____

## Birthday Chart

|  | Name | Birthday | Age |
|---|---|---|---|
| **January** | | | |
| **February** | | | |
| **March** | | | |
| **April** | | | |
| **May** | | | |
| **June** | | | |
| **July** | | | |
| **August** | | | |
| **September** | | | |
| **October** | | | |
| **November** | | | |
| **December** | | | |

## CHAPTER CHECKLIST

Yes    No

☐  ☐  Do you know who's who, what they do and how to contact them?
☐  ☐  District level?  School level?  Special education team?

☐  ☐  Do you have the school calendar?  School schedule?
☐  ☐  Do you know your daily teaching schedule?

☐  ☐  Do you have a staff handbook?
☐  ☐  Do you know what school policies are needed on the first day of school?

☐  ☐  Do you have classroom supplies, furniture and equipment?
☐  ☐  Do you know how to order materials from the district's curriculum library?
☐  ☐  Do you know what supplies/equipment you need to order?

☐  ☐  Have you arranged/organized your classroom?
☐  ☐  Have you set up your workspace?  Does your room function logically?

☐  ☐  Have you designed your bulletin boards?
☐  ☐  Do you have functional bulletin boards?

☐  ☐  Will you need to share a room with a colleague?

☐  ☐  Have you developed long-term curriculum plans?
☐  ☐  Have you considered how to organize/manage student information?
☐  ☐  Do you have a way to check the week at a glance?
☐  ☐  Can you track daily lessons and manage daily details?
☐  ☐  Do you know how to integrate curriculum units?

**Notes:**

# PLANNING THE FIRST DAYS OF SCHOOL

**Chapter 2**

**Starting school successfully requires thoughtful planning.**

## WHAT TO DO ON THE FIRST DAY OF SCHOOL

"What will I do on the first day of school?" This is a common question almost all students ask themselves. However, as you approach your first day of teaching, you are probably asking yourself exactly the same question!

What you do on the first day of school sets the tone for your classroom. This is the first time the students will see you in action. Research shows that students make decisions about a teacher's effectiveness within the first few minutes of the first day of class.

Fortunately, with thoughtful planning, your first day as teacher can be fun and academically successful for you and your students. This chapter reviews a number of concerns that must be considered as you prepare for the first day of school. Take a few minutes to think about some of these ideas. How do you plan to:

- ❖ Dress?

- ❖ Welcome your students?

- ❖ Assign seating?

- ❖ Introduce yourself?

- ❖ Begin to know your students?

- ❖ Teach?

- ❖ Communicate with parents?

*Trade Secrets*

## HOW DO YOU PLAN TO DRESS?

Dressing professionally models pride in your teaching position. However, what is considered professional dress may be somewhat different depending on the grade level you teach, school climate and the larger community in which the school is situated.

Present yourself to the students, parents and colleagues in a comfortable, yet professional outfit. Wear clothing appropriate to daily scheduled activities and in accordance with school/district policy. Some elementary teachers keep a large apron with pockets to use for special projects.

 Though the teacher's attire may become more business casual later in the year, most building administrators expect teachers to begin the year on a more conservative note.

 Wear a collared school-logo or school-colored shirt. Students will immediately identify you as a faculty member.

*Pockets are like extra hands.*

## HOW DO YOU PLAN TO WELCOME YOUR STUDENTS?

Your students need to feel welcome in your classroom. Many teachers use the children's names to decorate their doors. Likewise, primary teachers usually design and laminate unique name tags with sturdy strings to wear like necklaces. These novelty nametags may help both teacher and students immediately recognize members of their class. Stand by your door and greet the students as they enter your classroom.

*"We're the Stars!"*

 Name tags that have been laminated may be used throughout the year for field trips.

## HOW DO YOU PLAN TO ASSIGN SEATING?

Assigning seats helps teachers begin to learn their students' names and provides the students with a sense of knowing there is a place in the room that belongs to them. Assigned seating:

&#10070; Facilitates attendance taking during the first two weeks.

&#10070; Helps the teacher call students by name.

&#10070; Facilitates connecting names and faces.

**It's in the Cards -** Another way to assign seating involves a random activity called "Matching Cards." To conduct this activity the teacher needs two decks of playing cards. With one deck of cards the teacher quickly tapes one card to each desk. When the students arrive, the teacher hands each student a card from the second deck. Students then find their seat by matching cards. The teacher can then use the cards as a quick grouping strategy; for instance, "I need all the diamonds to line up," or "All the Kings can work in a group." An "Old Maid" deck of cards may also be used.

*Matching cards can be a fun, quick way to group students.*

 As you begin to learn more about your students, you may need to adjust the seating arrangements. Children with behavioral, visual or auditory challenges may need special considerations.

## HOW DO YOU PLAN TO INTRODUCE YOURSELF?

The first thing most students want to know is their teacher's name. In addition to writing your name on the board, you will want to introduce yourself in the manner you wish to be called; for example,

*"Good morning, I'm Mr. Black,"* or *"Welcome class, I'm Ms. Brown."*

Teachers who have a difficult last name to pronounce often give themselves a nickname; for instance,

*"Hello students. I'm Mrs. Debroucheckoffski, but you may call me Mrs. D."*

Students of all ages enjoy knowing something personal about their teachers on the first day of school. Personal information helps students relate to their teachers and actually reduces any anxieties they may have about you. You might share something about your family life, hobbies or pets. In addition, students may appreciate hearing something about your professional background; for instance, where you went to school and why you chose to teach this particular grade level. Many teachers display pictures of themselves, their families, pets and hobbies on a "Getting To Know You" bulletin board.

 Have you considered how you will introduce the instructional assistants and/or the resource teachers who work with you?

These individuals are an important part of your classroom community; their roles and responsibilities should be described also.

 Smile! Enthusiastically greet your students.

Your energy will motivate student learning and begin to build a positive classroom climate.

 Be sure that any personal information you share about yourself is appropriate. Likewise, as you begin to know your students, it will be important to appreciate their diverse cultural, linguistic and ethnic backgrounds.

*Trade Secrets*

## HOW DO YOU PLAN TO BEGIN TO KNOW YOUR STUDENTS?

Posting class rosters will help students find the right classroom. Name tags will help you connect names and faces. But these first steps do not include you "getting to know" your students. Learning about your students is one of your most critical responsibilities, and includes:

❖ Discovering interests, talents and skills.
❖ Becoming aware of home situations.
❖ Understanding unique learning styles.

Getting to know your students takes time and is not something that can be accomplished by the end of the first day of school. However, you can speed up this process by providing opportunities for students to get to know each other and learn about you. Students will enjoy introducing themselves by participating in one or more of the following activities.

**"Getting-to-Know-You" Graphing -** Give each child about six small sticky notes. Then begin to give directions; for example,

"We are going to make a footwear graph. If you are wearing shoes with buckles, write your name on the sticky note and place it on the graph. Look, Bart, Mary and James are all wearing shoes with a buckle."

Use several categories, such as sandals, loafers, shoes with buckles, shoestrings or velcro. Another day you could ask questions about pets, numbers of brothers and sisters or favorite foods.

## SHOE GRAPH

| Buckle | Ties | Sandal | Velcro | Tennis |
|---|---|---|---|---|
| Bart Mary James | Leonard Ashley Raul Tyler | Jennifer Michael Troy Geena Robbie | Stephen Phillip Summer Corey | Tammy Maria Jeremy Chuck Ethan |

*A Getting-To-Know-You Graph*

**Tasty Introductions -** Pass around a bag of M & Ms and ask students to take no more than six, but they can take less. They cannot eat them. Once all the students have M & Ms, instruct them that for each M & M they have, they must say one thing about themselves. The teacher should model this activity; for example, the teacher takes four M & Ms and demonstrates by stating four things about herself.

1. My name is Mrs. Ortiz.
2. I have a cat named Sasha.
3. I like to sew and make crafts.
4. My favorite food is Italian.

**All Wound Up -** Start with a piece of yarn about two feet long. Give to one student. As the student winds the yarn loosely around their hand, he/she shares appropriate personal information. When the yarn is all used, they must stop talking and pass the piece of yarn to the next student. This technique encourages quiet students to share more than just their name, and subtlety limits the amount of time some students could dominate the floor. The teacher should model this activity.

**Pair Shares -** Split students into pairs. Each pair has one minute to find five things they have in common. At the end of the minute, put two pairs together and give the foursome a minute to find thing(s) all four have in common. Finally, each group presents the list of things they have in common to the rest of the class. The teacher should model the type of information that is most appropriate; for instance:

❖ Favorite subject in school.
❖ Least favorite subject in school.
❖ Favorite kind of stories (mystery, biography, factual).
❖ Type of pet/s.
❖ Favorite television shows.
❖ Favorite movie.

**Scavenger Hunt -** Give each student the scavenger hunt list on page 62. Using inside voices, give students ten minutes to complete the list. The class then shares the names they have collected as the class debriefs.

 These "Getting-to-Know-You" activities may be used throughout the first few weeks of school to help build classroom community.

**Scavenger Hunt -** Find Someone Who:

Lived in another state _____

Speaks another language _____

Has more than two pets _____

Has visited Disneyland _____

Has more than three siblings _____

Is wearing more than two rings _____

Can do a cartwheel _____

Is named after a movie/TV star _____

Plays a sport _____

Plays a musical instrument _____

Wears the same size shoes that you wear _____

**Parent Perspective**

Another way to learn about your students is by contacting parents by phone or through the mail or email prior to the start of school. Parents are pleased that the teacher cares about their children and this action usually initiates a productive partnership that lasts all year long. Or, this survey could be completed at a " Meet the Teacher" night or sent home with the student on the first day of school. Parents may share valuable information that will help you meet your students' needs.

---

Dear Parent,

My name is Mrs. Cano. I am looking forward to being your child's teacher. Since your child's learning, happiness and health are so important to me, I am asking you to read and complete the following questions and return this form. I look forward to getting to know both you and your child better.

Child's Name *Jennifer Vandush* Age *6* Date of Birth *January 21, 1995*

Parent Names *Claudia and John Vandush*

Phone: Home *(480) 926-4287* Work *(623) 246-5376* E-mail *JVandush@email.org*

1. How will your child be transported to and from school? *school bus*

2. How is your child's overall health? *Good, but she does have asthma.*

3. Are there health concerns that I should know about?
   Food allergies? Colds? Ear infections? *No*

4. List any medication your child takes regularly. *Inhaler as needed*

5. How many hours of sleep a night does your child usually get? *9 hours*

6. List the names and ages of your other children. *2 other children*

   *Brian      7 years old*
   *Amanda     3 years old*

7. What activities does your child enjoy the most? The least? *Jennifer enjoys sports. She likes to swing and play with her friends. Jennifer does not like playing by herself, she enjoys the company of others.*

8. What languages are spoken in the home? *English*

9. What are your child's favorite TV shows? Movies? *Sailor Moon and Dr. Doolittle*

10. What is the title of your child's favorite book? *Corduroy*

11. Are there other concerns or things that I should know about? *No*

---

## *Parent Survey Template*

Dear Parent,

I am looking forward to being your child's teacher. Since your child's learning, happiness and health are so important to me, I am asking you to read and complete the following questions and return this form. I look forward to getting to know both you and your child better.

Child's Name _____ Age _____ Date of Birth _____
Parent Names _____
Phone: Home _____ Work _____ Email _____

1. How will your child be transported to and from school?

2. How is your child's overall health?

3. Are there health concerns that I should know about?
   Food allergies? Colds? Ear infections?

4. List any medication your child takes regularly.

5. How many hours of sleep a night does your child usually get?

6. List the names and ages of your other children.

7. What activities does your child enjoy the most? The least?

8. What languages are spoken in the home?

9. What are your child's favorite TV shows? Movies?

10. What is the title of your child's favorite book?

11. Are there other concerns or things that I should know about?

### Additional Parent Survey Example

Dear Parents:

I'd like to know more about your son/daughter, through your eyes. The more I know, the better I can tailor an educational and motivational program to fit his/her particular needs. Please answer the questions and complete the information below. Remember, this is from your point of view. I will discuss the same information with your son/daughter.

Son/Daughter's Name **Jonathan Jeffries**

1. List five words that best describe your son/daughter's character. He is creative, imaginative, outgoing, friendly and easygoing.

2. What motivates your son/daughter? Jonathan is motivated by interest and hands-on experiences.

3. What upsets your son/daughter? Jonathan gets frustrated easily when he has a hard time understanding ideas and concepts.

4. What are your son/daughter's out-of-school interests and activities? Jonathan plays Little League Baseball and enjoys video games.

5. What activities do you share? We have one night a week set aside for meaningful family activities. As a family we enjoying camping, fishing and going to the park.

6. How would you describe your son/daughter's study habits? We try hard to instill the importance of education in our children. When they come home from school, homework is to be completed before any other activities.

7. What study skills does your son/daughter need to develop? Jonathan needs help with memorization and skimming skills.

8. What are your son/daughter's favorite subjects? Most challenging? Jonathan's favorite subjects are science and reading. (Although he tells us recess and lunch.) He struggles in spelling and math.

9. What particular academic areas would you like to see emphasized? I would like reading to be emphasized and I would like to see Jonathan excel in math and science.

10. What social skills would you like to see developed? I would like to see teamwork and cooperation skills developed.

11. Are there any personal or physical problems I should know about? No

12. Would you like a personal conference? Not at this time

13. Other comments or concerns? None

Parent signature(s) Allison Jeffries

## *Parent Survey Template*

Dear Parents:

I'd like to know more about your son/daughter, through your eyes. The more I know, the better I can tailor an educational and motivational program to fit his/her particular needs. Please answer the questions and complete the information below. Remember, this is from your point of view. I will discuss the same information with your son/daughter.

Son/Daughter's Name _____

1.  List five words that best describe your son/daughter's character.


2.  What motivates your son/daughter?


3.  What upsets your son/daughter?


4.  What are your son/daughter's out-of-school interests and activities?


5.  What activities do you share?


6.  How would you describe your son/daughter's study habits?


7.  What study skills does your son/daughter need to develop?


8.  What are your son/daughter's favorite subjects?          Most challenging?


9.  What particular academic areas would you like to see emphasized?


10.  What social skills would you like to see developed?


11.  Are there any personal or physical problems I should know about?


12.  Would you like a personal conference?


13.  Other comments or concerns?


Parent signature(s) _____

### Preview of Coming Attractions

If you are able to obtain an address list of your students a week or two prior to the start of the school, you could send them a "preview of coming attractions" letter. This type of communication could begin the process of building a learning community. The following is an example of this type of letter.

---

Dear Third Grader and Family,

Welcome back!!! I am very excited about the upcoming school year. I am Mrs. Marbles and I am looking forward to being your third grade teacher! Third grade is an exciting year, and we have many challenging and fun learning adventures ahead of us.

Before school begins, I want you to know a little about me. I enjoy hiking, swimming and tennis. One of my favorite passions is reading!!! In our class we will be using great literature to study content across the curriculum. For instance, during the first week of school we will use the story line from the book, *The Patchwork Quilt,* to help us begin to build a strong classroom community.

Now that you know a little about me, I am looking forward to getting to know each of you!!! I hope to see you and your family at "Meet Your Teacher Night" (Wednesday, August 18th from 5 - 7:00 p.m.). As an extended classroom community, we are about to embark on a learning adventure together. It will be exciting, fun and challenging. I look forward to seeing how you will learn and grow this year. As a team, I know that we can make great things happen.

Happy to be your teacher,

Mrs. Marbles

P.S. We have adopted a classroom pet! See if you can guess, from these clues, what kind of animal he is. " I am cute, furry, about nine inches in length, and I am three inches tall. I like to eat grains, fruits and vegetables. I don't have much of a tail, but you can't help but notice my whiskers. Most of all, I love third graders. What kind of animal am I?"

---

More ways to learn about your students:

 Teachers can and should see their students in a variety of contexts. Attend a music class with your students or participate in a PE class. When you do not have duty, visit the playground; students notice who plays with whom. What activities do your students engage in or shy away from?

 Personal two-way interactive journals are an effective way to get to know your students both personally and academically.

It is important for primary teachers to respond to their students' journals as soon as possible.

Students also find it exciting to eat lunch with their teachers.

Plan a weekly or bimonthly "Eat with the Teacher" day. Younger students may bring sack lunches.

*Sharing meals together allows time to talk and learn about each other.*

## HOW DO YOU PLAN TO COMMUNICATE WITH PARENTS?

**First Day Communiqué -** During the opening day of school you have a perfect opportunity to introduce yourself, establish expectations and routine procedures, and ask for parental support. The first day communiqué to the parents should introduce you as the teacher, describe some feature of the learning activities the students will experience in your class, review classroom expectations, and encourage parents to contact you if they have questions. Your communiqué might refer to the principal's "Welcome" newsletter, which often includes information about school hours, bus schedules, attendance policies and procedures, and cafeteria information.

Regardless of what you write about, the tone of your communiqué should be friendly. All information should be stated in a positive manner; for example, "Students need to wear comfortable clothes to school," not "Students should not wear dress clothes to school."

 Your first written communiqué will make a lasting impression. Have a colleague or your mentor edit your work for grammar, spelling, and, most importantly, a positive "tone."

 In some schools the principal will need to approve all communications.

In other schools, principals only want a copy of your letter. Be sure to inquire about the policy at your school.

 To be sure the first day communiqué is read by parents, include a detachable and returnable portion for parent signature and responses. An example of a first day communiqué for a primary classroom is presented on page 71.

**Back-to-School Kit -** The first day communiqué could be part of a "Back-to-School" Kit, which includes:

- ❖ The principal's newsletter.

- ❖ Information about the parent-teacher organization.

- ❖ The school's menu for the month.

- ❖ A form that updates parents' home and work information.

- ❖ An emergency form that identifies other adults who may serve as guardian in an emergency.

- ❖ A list of supplies needed for school.

- ❖ A "Getting To Know Your Child" questionnaire (if you have not had an opportunity to send this survey prior to the beginning of the school year.) (See pages 60-66 for more information.)

 Students will enter your classroom throughout the year. To assist their families adjust to a new school, make 12-15 extra Back-to-School Kits.

**Welcome**
**Parents & Students**

Please read and respond as requested:
- ❖ Principal's newsletter
- ❖ Parent organization
- ❖ August – September menu
- ❖ Update forms
- ❖ Emergency forms
- ❖ School supplies

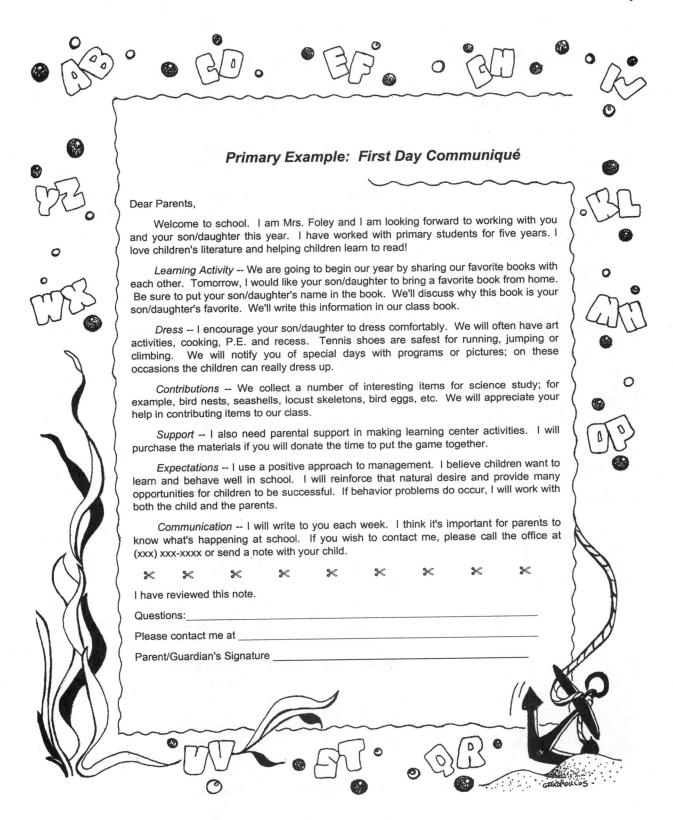

## Primary Example: First Day Communiqué

Dear Parents,

Welcome to school. I am Mrs. Foley and I am looking forward to working with you and your son/daughter this year. I have worked with primary students for five years. I love children's literature and helping children learn to read!

*Learning Activity* -- We are going to begin our year by sharing our favorite books with each other. Tomorrow, I would like your son/daughter to bring a favorite book from home. Be sure to put your son/daughter's name in the book. We'll discuss why this book is your son/daughter's favorite. We'll write this information in our class book.

*Dress* -- I encourage your son/daughter to dress comfortably. We will often have art activities, cooking, P.E. and recess. Tennis shoes are safest for running, jumping or climbing. We will notify you of special days with programs or pictures; on these occasions the children can really dress up.

*Contributions* -- We collect a number of interesting items for science study; for example, bird nests, seashells, locust skeletons, bird eggs, etc. We will appreciate your help in contributing items to our class.

*Support* -- I also need parental support in making learning center activities. I will purchase the materials if you will donate the time to put the game together.

*Expectations* -- I use a positive approach to management. I believe children want to learn and behave well in school. I will reinforce that natural desire and provide many opportunities for children to be successful. If behavior problems do occur, I will work with both the child and the parents.

*Communication* -- I will write to you each week. I think it's important for parents to know what's happening at school. If you wish to contact me, please call the office at (xxx) xxx-xxxx or send a note with your child.

✂    ✂    ✂    ✂    ✂    ✂    ✂    ✂    ✂

I have reviewed this note.

Questions:_____

Please contact me at _____

Parent/Guardian's Signature _____

## WHAT DO YOU PLAN TO TEACH?

Planning lessons for the first day of school involves knowing exactly:

❖ What you want to do.
❖ What materials you need.

❖ When you need to do it.
❖ How to do what needs to be done.

Consider your day in 15-minute blocks of time. This tight timeframe encourages you to over-plan. This is important since students tend to work quickly and teachers tend to instruct faster on the first day of school.

Remember that a large part of your first day will revolve around meeting your students and establishing classroom routines and expectations. "The First Day Form" on the following page is designed to help you consider first day and week activities in 15-minute time periods. Consider how you will:

❖ Meet students at the door.
❖ Greet students and introduce yourself.
❖ Have a prepared seating chart.
❖ Take attendance and ask students to clarify name pronunciation.
❖ Do a get-acquainted activity.
❖ Discuss classroom policies and procedures.
❖ Discuss the school-wide discipline plan.
❖ Conduct an exciting activity to set the tone for the year.
❖ Issue textbooks (if necessary).
❖ Establish a dismissal routine that emphasizes neatness and orderliness.

In addition to teaching procedures, it is very important to schedule time during the first day for engaging students in real content work. This will give the students a look into what is to come and something specific to communicate when their parents ask, "What did you learn today?"

❖ Be sure to block out special classes, lunch period, recesses and dismissal times. Plan to leave at least five minutes early for these activities; use the time to practice lining up, walking in line and reviewing new rules.

❖ Your demeanor and expectations on this day will affect students' behavior for the entire year.

**Opening Day Plan -** Every district/school may have essential tasks for the first day so be sure to ask your grade level chair, mentor or colleague.

**The First Day Form**

| Time | Strategy: What I Will Do? | Activity: What Will Students Do? | Materials Needed? | Management Considerations? |
|------|---------------------------|----------------------------------|-------------------|----------------------------|
|      |                           |                                  |                   |                            |
|      |                           |                                  |                   |                            |
|      |                           |                                  |                   |                            |
|      |                           |                                  |                   |                            |
|      |                           |                                  |                   |                            |
|      |                           |                                  |                   |                            |
|      |                           |                                  |                   |                            |
|      |                           |                                  |                   |                            |
|      |                           |                                  |                   |                            |
|      |                           |                                  |                   |                            |
|      |                           |                                  |                   |                            |

*Trade Secrets*

**Notes:**

**Section B**

## ESTABLISHING MANAGEMENT ROUTINES

All classrooms have routine tasks and procedures that must be performed on a daily basis. Well-developed routines serve as management tools, save time and ensure a smooth functioning classroom. Recommended strategies for success:

❖ Identify effective daily routine tasks.

❖ Determine when to teach these routine tasks.

❖ Analyze each task and plan how it will be taught.

Experienced teachers and classroom-effectiveness researchers suggest that the establishment of these routines should begin on the first day and continue through at least the first two weeks of school. Classroom management experts stress that using this time to teach routines will actually give you more total teaching time during the year, plus the benefit of having a well-managed, organized classroom (Wong & Wong, 1991; Kronowitz, 1996).

*Clearly established routines and classroom jobs ensure an effective, organized and well-managed classroom.*

## DETERMINING ROUTINE TASKS

There are virtually dozens of routine tasks that could make classroom life easier and more organized. The following list offers a number of routines and procedures that are used in effective classrooms. Many of these routines are described on the following pages.

### Beginning Class

___Enter/Exiting the Classroom
___Attention Signal
___Attendance Procedures
___Lunch Count
___Tardy Students

### Grading and Checking Assignments

___ Self-Checked Work
___ Editing Checklist
___ Grading Criteria/Rubrics
___ Recording Grades

### Classroom Management Procedures

___Rules of Respect
___Out-of-Room Policies
___Restroom Procedures
___Drinking Fountain
___Pencil Sharpening
___Fire/Earthquake/Bomb Threat Drills
___Noise Control
___Movement in Classroom

### Work Expectations and Requirements

___ Heading Papers
___ Name/Number/Class Information
___ Quality of Work
___ Incomplete/Incorrect Work
___ Turning in Completed Work
___Homework Check-In

### Instructional Activities

___Assignment Calendar
___Distributing Supplies
___Seeking Teacher's Help
___Storing/Filing Work
___Computer Access
___Finishing Work Early
___Study Buddy System

### Transitions and Dismissing Class

___ Putting Away Supplies and Equipment
___ Cleaning Up
___ Going to Special Support Services,
    Speech and Resource
___ Lining Up and Moving In Line

## WHAT ROUTINES WILL I TEACH DURING THE FIRST WEEK OF SCHOOL?

After you decide what routines you need, you will need to determine when you will teach them.

It is important to teach routine procedures in context. For example, you teach lining-up procedures the first time you need to take your students out of the classroom.

The first column provides a sample of the way one elementary teacher taught the routines in her class. The second column is a place for you to consider what you plan to do.

Reorder the sample below to match your teaching in context.

| | |
|---|---|
| **Monday**<br>Attention Signal<br>Lunch Count Routine<br>Lining Up and Moving In Line<br>Rules of Respect<br>Entering/Exiting the Classroom | **Monday** |
| **Tuesday**<br>Attendance Procedures<br>Bathroom Procedures<br>Distributing Supplies<br>Turning In Completed Work | **Tuesday** |
| **Wednesday**<br>Pencil Sharpening<br>Drinking Fountain<br>Noise Control<br>Study Buddy System | **Wednesday** |
| **Thursday**<br>Finishing Work Early<br>Seeking Teacher's Help<br>Fire/Earthquake/Bomb Threat Drill<br>Storing and Filing Work | **Thursday** |
| **Friday**<br>Classroom Jobs<br>Learning-Center Behavior<br>End-of-Day Cleanup | **Friday** |

## TASK ANALYSIS AND TEACHING ROUTINE TASKS

After you have identified which routine tasks you need and when to teach them, you will need to analyze the routine to decide how to teach routines most efficiently. There are basically two steps in task analysis:

1. *What is the rationale of the procedure to be learned?*

2. *What are the logical steps needed to learn the procedure?*

Following are examples of task analysis and explicit directions on how to teach the most basic routines.

### *Attention Signal* (Also see Chapter 3.)

1. *What is the rationale of the procedure to be learned?*

   The teacher needs to be able to obtain students' attention quickly.

2. *What are the logical steps needed to learn the procedure?*

   **Information and Modeling -** "When I need you to be quiet, I will tap on the bell three times. When you hear the signal, you're to stop what you are doing, stop talking and listen for directions."

   **Guided Practice -** "Let's practice. Talk to your neighbor for a minute." [After a minute the teachers taps the bell three times.] "Good, everyone has stopped talking and is listening for the next direction."

   **Check for Understanding -** Observe the class as they learn the new routine. Reteach immediately if there are misunderstandings. Initially, be sure you thank students for completing routine tasks successfully.

 Nonverbal, visual signals are another category of attention signals.

Silent signals speak volumes and clearly communicate your message in an instant, if you teach their meaning. Here are some examples:

❖ Five-finger countdown.
❖ Facial expression and eye contact.
❖ Physical proximity.
❖ Switch light off and on.

 Be willing to reteach procedures throughout the year as the need arises.

*Leaving the Room*

**1.**   ***What is the rationale of the procedure to be learned?***

The teacher needs to know where all students are every moment of the day.

**2.**   ***What are the logical steps needed to learn the procedure?***

**Information and Modeling -** When a student needs to go to the bathroom or special class, they need to go with a partner.  They take their name clip from the class clip chart and place it beside their destination.  When the students return to class, they replace their name clips on the class clip chart.

**Guided Practice -** "Sharon needs to take a note to the office.  Sharon, show the class what you need to do." As Sharon models the procedure, the teacher narrates.  The teacher will need to demonstrate this process two or three times.

**Check for Understanding -** Observe the class as they learn the new routine.  Re-teach immediately if there are misunderstandings.  Initially, be sure to thank students for completing routine tasks successfully.

" I Am Here" Chart

**Name Clip Chart**

### *Lining Up and Moving In Line*

**1.  What is the rationale of the procedure to be learned?**

Throughout the day primary teachers will need to quickly and safely transport their students to other classes and activities.

**2.  What are the logical steps needed to learn the procedure?**

**Information and Modeling -** "When you line up, you need to stand and walk quietly behind the person in front of you.  Listen, keep your hands by your sides and watch where the line is going."

**Guided Practice -** "Everyone who is sitting at table one may line up. Let's see if table one can follow directions.  Good, they got in line quickly but safely." The teacher will need to practice this routine with all tables.

**Check for Understanding -** Teachers will need to observe students lining up and walking in line.  This routine is somewhat challenging for younger students. Observe the class as they learn the new routines.  Re-teach routine immediately if there are misunderstandings.

There are many interesting ways to help your students get in a line.  The following "Simon Says" ideas are both fun and help students listen carefully. Line up if you:

Have a missing tooth.
Are wearing a striped shirt, a blue shirt...
Have a ribbon (bow, headband) in your hair.
Have a "B" in your name, a "D"...
Are wearing buckled shoes, tennis shoes.
Have two (three, four, ten) people in your family.
Own a pet dog, cat, bird, hamster...
Have a birthday in May, June...
Brought your library book back today.
Have hair longer than your teacher, shorter than...
Have blue eyes, green, brown, hazel...

 As you teach procedures be as specific as possible.

Specific feedback facilitates greater understanding of the routine tasks.

 Leave for lunch (or special class) a few minutes early during the first week. Students need time to practice walking in line safely and quietly.

*Talk Light*

1.  *What is the rationale of the procedure to be learned?*

The students need to learn to adjust their volume in accordance with different activities.

2.  *What are the logical steps needed to learn the procedure?*

**Information and Modeling -** The teacher will need to introduce the talk light. "When the talk light is set on red, you need to be completely quiet, no talking. When do you think the talk light should be on red?" Students and teacher generate a list of silent times. The teacher and students then discuss activities that are appropriate for the yellow light talk, which indicates time for soft talking. Students may practice soft talking to confirm the quality of that volume. Finally, the class discusses green light activities and volume.

**Guided Practice -** As the students get ready to do an activity, the teacher will ask, "How should we set the talk light?" The teacher confirms the volume level.

**Check for Understanding -** Teachers will need to observe students as they work. If the volume is inappropriate, the teacher can comment, "Show me how you should talk when the talk light is set on yellow." Observe the class as they learn the new routine. Re-teach routine if there are misunderstandings.

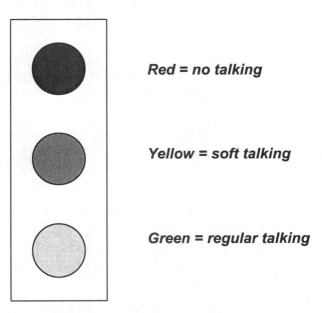

*Red = no talking*

*Yellow = soft talking*

*Green = regular talking*

### *Study Buddy System*

1. ***What is the rationale of the procedure to be learned?***

Students who are absent (part of a day or full day) need information about what was missed.

2. ***What are the logical steps needed to learn the procedure?***

**Information and Modeling -** The teacher will need to help students establish a study buddy team. There are two options: The buddies exchange phone numbers and addresses. The teacher makes a master list. When a student is absent, the buddy completes a "While You Were Out" form. That night the absent buddy calls the study buddy and receives the assignments and information they missed. Study buddy meets with absent student prior to class.

**Guided Practice -** After the buddies have been paired, the teacher reviews the procedure. Next, the teacher asks one-half of the buddy team to stand outside the door. Then the teacher gives a fun assignment so the other half of the team can practice completing the "While You Were Out" form. The teacher then switches the buddies, giving the second group a completely different assignment. That night or the next morning the buddies practice sharing the information. The following day the teacher collects both sets of assignments to see how well the buddies shared information.

**Check for Understanding -** The teacher reviews the assignments to determine how well each buddy transmitted information.

| Name: Sally | Class: 2nd Grade | Date: 10-3 |
| --- | --- | --- |
| Assignments: Remember to bring field trip note | | |
| Practice for spelling test | | |

Assign a weekly study buddy monitor who distributes forms to the study buddy of absent students. The master study buddy list is posted in the room for easy referral.

*Your Turn: Work Through a Task Analysis and Teaching a Routine Task*

**Procedure:**

1. *What is the rational of the procedure to be learned?*

2. *What are the logical steps needed to learn the procedure?*

**Information and Modeling**

**Guided Practice**

**Check for Understanding**

 Ask questions of mentor teachers.

Get their advice about how to conduct the first visit to the lunchroom or music teacher.

 Take time to teach routines and practice until students know and can do each routine well.

*Trade Secrets*

## Notes:

# LIGHTENING THE LOAD: STUDENT JOBS

As you can see by the examples on the previous pages, routine tasks are explicitly taught by the teacher. However, many daily routines can and should be maintained by the students in your class. After determining, analyzing, teaching, and establishing management routines, your next step is to decide what tasks you can delegate to students in your room.

## DETERMINING STUDENT JOBS

Beyond making classroom life easier for the teacher, classroom jobs build ownership and pride in the classroom. Students enjoy assisting. The following is a list of possible classroom jobs. Some jobs are more primary, while others are appropriate for older students.

| | |
|---|---|
| Class Secretary | Assignment Manager |
| Paper Passer | Study Buddy Monitor |
| Packet Makers | Lunch Chart Recorder |
| Classroom Librarian | Line Leader |
| Pencil Sharpener | Errand Runner |

Whatever jobs you decide to assign, be sure students complete their responsibilities. Teach specifically the job details. You will save hours of time and have a well-managed, organized, and positive classroom that compliments both you and your students.

 After you have taught the first assistants their jobs, they can be responsible for teaching the next person the details of that specific duty. This saves even more time.

## TASK ANALYSIS AND TEACHING STUDENT JOBS

After you have identified which student jobs you need, you will need to analyze the job to decide how to teach it. Like routine tasks, there are basically two steps in task analysis.

### *Pencil Sharpener*

1.   *What is the rationale of the procedure to be learned?*

Students always have sharpened pencils available for use without disrupting class time. He/ she places them in the pencil exchange can points up.

2.   *What are the logical steps needed to learn the procedure?*

**Information and Modeling -** The pencil sharpener collects the dull pencils and sharpens them during the last five minutes of class time. He/she places them in the pencil exchange can points up.

**Guided Practice –** Students turn in dull pencils to pencil can. Pencil sharpener implement procedure.

**Check for Understanding -** Teacher will need to observe students using this routine. Re-teach routine if there are misunderstandings.

**Homework Manager**

**1.** ***What is the goal of the procedure to be learned?***

Homework manager checks in homework as required.

**2.** ***What are the logical steps needed to learn the procedure?***

**Information and Modeling** – The homework manager sorts turned in homework chronologically and/or alphabetically and submits ordered papers to teacher assigned area.

**Guided Practice** – Student submits homework. The homework manager implements procedure.

**Check for Understanding** – After the homework manager has checked in assignments, the teacher periodically checks routine.

| Activity: Homework | | | | | | | Date: Oct. 2-6 |
|---|---|---|---|---|---|---|---|
| Student Code | Name | M | T | W | Th | F | Notes |
| 1 | Bob A. | | | | | | |
| 2 | Bob B. | | | | | | |
| 3 | Karen C. | | | | | | |
| 4 | Don E. | | | | | | |
| 5 | Kelly F. | | | | | | |
| 6 | Connie G. | | | | | | |
| 7 | Howard H. | | | | | | |
| 8 | Brian J. | | | | | | |
| 9 | Darcy K. | | | | | | |
| 10 | Cal L. | | | | | | |
| | | | | | | | |

*Trade Secrets*

## Generic Check-In Form

Sometimes you will be collecting forms, money and permission slips simultaneously. The multi-purpose chart is extremely helpful to keep track of multiple activities. Be sure to place student names/code in the first column. Make 20-30 copies for easy use. For example:

| Student Code # | Name | Field Trip | Photo $ | Conference Form | | | | Notes |
|---|---|---|---|---|---|---|---|---|
| 1 | Bob A. | √ | √ | √ | | | | |
| 2 | Bob B. | √ | √ | √ | | | | |
| 3 | Karen C. | √ | | √ | | | | |
| 4 | Don E. | √ | | √ | | | | |
| 5 | Kelly F. | √ | √ | √ | | | | |
| 6 | Carrie G. | | | √ | | | | |
| 7 | Howard H. | √ | √ | | | | | |
| 8 | Brian J. | | √ | | | | | |
| 9 | Darcy K. | √ | √ | √ | | | | |
| 10 | Cal L. | √ | | | | | | |

**FORMS**

### *Generic Daily Check-In Form*

Activity_____Date_____

| Student Code | Name/s | M | T | W | Th | F | Notes |
|---|---|---|---|---|---|---|---|
| 1 | | | | | | | |
| 2 | | | | | | | |
| 3 | | | | | | | |
| 4 | | | | | | | |
| 5 | | | | | | | |
| 6 | | | | | | | |
| 7 | | | | | | | |
| 8 | | | | | | | |
| 9 | | | | | | | |
| 10 | | | | | | | |
| 11 | | | | | | | |
| 12 | | | | | | | |
| 13 | | | | | | | |
| 14 | | | | | | | |
| 15 | | | | | | | |
| 16 | | | | | | | |
| 17 | | | | | | | |
| 18 | | | | | | | |
| 19 | | | | | | | |
| 20 | | | | | | | |
| 21 | | | | | | | |
| 22 | | | | | | | |
| 23 | | | | | | | |
| 24 | | | | | | | |
| 25 | | | | | | | |
| 26 | | | | | | | |
| 27 | | | | | | | |
| 28 | | | | | | | |
| 29 | | | | | | | |
| 30 | | | | | | | |

## *Multi-Purpose Chart*

Date_____

| Student Code | Name | | | | | | | | Notes |
|---|---|---|---|---|---|---|---|---|---|
| 1 | | | | | | | | | |
| 2 | | | | | | | | | |
| 3 | | | | | | | | | |
| 4 | | | | | | | | | |
| 5 | | | | | | | | | |
| 6 | | | | | | | | | |
| 7 | | | | | | | | | |
| 8 | | | | | | | | | |
| 9 | | | | | | | | | |
| 10 | | | | | | | | | |
| 11 | | | | | | | | | |
| 12 | | | | | | | | | |
| 13 | | | | | | | | | |
| 14 | | | | | | | | | |
| 15 | | | | | | | | | |
| 16 | | | | | | | | | |
| 17 | | | | | | | | | |
| 18 | | | | | | | | | |
| 19 | | | | | | | | | |
| 20 | | | | | | | | | |
| 21 | | | | | | | | | |
| 22 | | | | | | | | | |
| 23 | | | | | | | | | |
| 24 | | | | | | | | | |
| 25 | | | | | | | | | |
| 26 | | | | | | | | | |
| 27 | | | | | | | | | |
| 28 | | | | | | | | | |
| 29 | | | | | | | | | |
| 30 | | | | | | | | | |

**Section D**

# LIGHTENING THE LOAD: PARENT HELPERS

Student jobs are one of the most effective ways to lighten your load. Another excellent source of help is parent volunteers. There are many ways parents can make contributions to the classroom and save you dozens of hours weekly.

## DETERMINING PARENTAL TASKS

**Party Planners -** Help by planning and managing classroom celebrations throughout the year. One parent may wish to take the lead for each party. These parents and grandparents usually make a two to three-hour time commitment about four times a year.

**Parent Tutors -** Work with children in small groups or tutor one-to-one. This type of parental role requires parents who are willing to make consistent weekly commitments. These parents and grandparents should be willing to spend time planning and debriefing with the teachers.

**Parent Helpers -** Help classroom by preparing learning games, grading and recording students' work, creating bulletin boards, etc. These parents and grandparents should make monthly or bimonthly time commitments.

**At-Home Helpers -** Support classroom teacher by preparing games, creating bulletin boards, organizing/managing book orders, etc. These parents and grandparents need to respond to time deadlines but may work at home to complete tasks.

 Whatever parent jobs you decide on, be sure to help parents and grandparents complete their tasks successfully the first time. For instance, it will be necessary to demonstrate how to use the copier, work the laminator or place a book order.

### *Sample Parent Volunteer Letter*

Dear Parents,

We have many wonderful learning activities planned this year. I would appreciate any help you could offer our classroom. Please place a check by the task you are interested in and complete the bottom section of this letter.

____*Party Planner* - Plans and manages classroom celebrations throughout the year. One parent may wish to take the lead for each party. These parents or grandparents usually make a two to three-hour time commitment about four times a year.

____*Parent Tutor* - Work with students in small groups or tutor one-to-one. This type of parental role requires parents who are willing to make consistent weekly commitments. These parents or grandparents should be willing to spend time planning and debriefing with the teachers.

____*Parent Helper* - Prepares learning games, grades and records student's work, creates bulletin boards, etc. These parents or grandparents usually make monthly or bimonthly time commitments.

____*At-Home Helper* - Prepares games, creates bulletin boards, organizes and manages book orders, etc. These parents or grandparents need to respond to time deadlines but may work at home to complete tasks.

Name_____ Phone_____Email_____

Address_____

Best time to reach you_____

Questions or Concerns?_____

Please identify activities you are especially interested in_____

_____

## GUIDELINES FOR PARENTAL VOLUNTEERS

Once you have determined what capacity parents or grandparents are interested in, it is time to conduct "Job Alike" workshops. If you have two or three parents who wish to be "Parent Helpers" or "At-Home Parent Helpers," ask them to meet with you for an hour after school. At this time you can review the specifics of certain tasks you will be asking them to complete.

Beyond sharing the "how-to-do-its," it is also time to review school policies and discuss any questions they might have.

- ❖ Do they need to sign in at the office?
- ❖ Do they need to wear nametags?
- ❖ Where do they park?
- ❖ Can they bring younger children?

 It is important to remind parents about maintaining students' confidentiality.

*Parents provide extra hands*
*to share workload and*
*special talents to enrich student learning.*

| Parent Helper | Phone # | Parent Helper | At-Home Helper | Party Planner | Parent Tutor | Notes |
|---|---|---|---|---|---|---|
| Mrs. Smith | (XXX) XXX–XXXX | | | ✓ | ✓ M * | Fall Party |
| Mr. Turner | (XXX) XXX–XXXX | ✓T* 11:00 | | | | Likes to do graphics and science |
| Mrs. Valdez | (XXX) XXX–XXXX | ✓ | | | | |
| Mrs. Marks | (XXX) XXX–XXXX | | | ✓ | | Winter party |
| Mrs. Eggs | (XXX) XXX–XXXX | ✓ T* | | ✓ F* | | Valentine's Day |
| Mrs. Jones | (XXX) XXX–XXXX | | ✓ | | | |

\* Denotes day  parents are available to work

Keeping track of your parent help requires a little organization.  A simple form can condense all the information on one-quick glance page.  This form can be kept in your planner. For example:  Mrs. Smith wants to work as a private tutor on Monday.  She also wishes to help plan the Fall party.   Mr. Turner wants to be an in-class parent helper.  He is good with graphics and enjoys science activities.  He is available from 11:00 a.m. until 4:00 p.m.

**CHAPTER CHECKLIST**

Take a few minutes to review your readiness for the first day of school.

Yes No    Do you know how you will:

☐ ☐    Assign seats?

☐ ☐    Introduce yourself?

☐ ☐    Conduct a "Getting to Know You" activity?

☐ ☐    Learn about students' interests and health concerns?

☐ ☐    Teach routine tasks?

☐ ☐    Take your students to lunch? (See Teacher Handbook or talk to colleague)

Yes No    Have you developed:         Yes No    Have you considered how:

☐ ☐    Name tags?                  ☐ ☐    To share classroom responsibilities?

☐ ☐    The first day communiqué?   ☐ ☐    To involve parents in the classroom?

☐ ☐    A list of classroom jobs?

☐ ☐    Back-to-school kits?

Yes No    Do you know:

☐ ☐    The school's rules?  (See Teacher Handbook)

☐ ☐    Emergency procedures? (See Teacher Handbook)

☐ ☐    How to plan for the first day of school?

## Notes:

Chapter 3

# CREATING A COOPERATIVE COMMUNITY

**How a child responds in the classroom
depends on the type of classroom environment you create.**

# BUILDING A FOUNDATION FOR MANAGEMENT

To build a house you need a firm foundation with carefully thought-out plans, good building materials and dedicated workmanship. Building a positive classroom climate also requires thoughtful planning and a skilled teacher. The teacher must simultaneously consider a number of building blocks that must be carefully placed into a management framework.

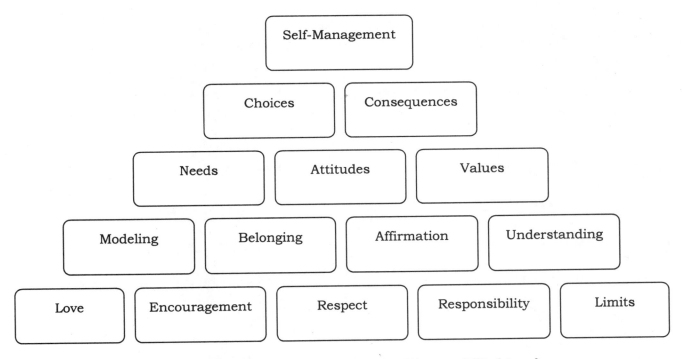

**Building a positive classroom community takes a skilled teacher and many thoughtfully considered building blocks.**

This chapter will address how students' primary personalities and psychological needs influence a teacher's choice and use of classroom management systems. It will also provide specific management strategies for primary and elementary classrooms.

## KNOW YOUR STUDENTS

Research has consistently shown that students learn more effectively and behave better in classrooms where personal and psychological needs are met. As you get to know your students, you will develop an understanding of their personality needs and interaction styles. This knowledge will help you proactively provide for varying needs and effectively resolve behavioral problems. The Array Management Model (Kortman, 1999), based on the Array Interaction Model (Knaupp, 1995), provides a way for you to orchestrate the management of your classroom by learning about your students' personalities and, in turn, helping you to understand why students behave as they do. Ultimately, this knowledge will help you respond to the unique needs of your students and provide a classroom community that equips students to self-manage themselves in positive ways.

### *Interaction Styles - Positive or Negative?*

The three most common interaction modes observed in the classroom setting are Cooperative, Marginal and Reluctant. A person acting in a Cooperative interaction mode is *positive, agreeable, helpful and collaborative*. The Marginal mode of interaction describes a person who is *neutral in attitudes and disengaged in interactions*. The Reluctant mode of interaction describes a student who is *involved, but in a negative way*. The following chart lists common behaviors observed when students are in either Cooperative or Reluctant behaviors.

| Cooperative Behavior | Reluctant Behavior |
| --- | --- |
| ❖ asks questions | ❖ gets angry, verbally aggressive |
| ❖ works toward goals | ❖ demands perfection |
| ❖ initiates work | ❖ feels inadequate, is self-defeating |
| ❖ cares about others | ❖ over-adapts |
| ❖ is enthusiastic | ❖ draws attention to self |
| ❖ interacts well with others | ❖ blames |
| ❖ is attentive | ❖ is disruptive |
| ❖ is eager to contribute | ❖ withdraws |

### *Personal Objectives/Personality Components*

Teacher and student personalities are a critical element in the classroom dynamic. The Array Interaction Model identifies four personality components called "Personal Objectives." All people have all four components; however, one or two are more prominent and tend to greatly influence the way a person sees the world and responds to it. A person whose primary Personal Objective is Harmony is feeling-oriented, and is caring and sensitive. A person with a primary Personal Objective of Production is organized, logical and thinking-oriented. A person whose primary Personal Objective is Connection is enthusiastic, spontaneous and action-oriented. A person whose primary Personal Objective is Status Quo is insightful, reflective and observant. The following figure presents the Array Interaction Model descriptors, offers specific Cooperative and Reluctant behaviors from each Personal Objective, and addresses needs associated with each in a classroom setting.

### Array Interaction Model

| | Personal Objectives/Personality Component | | | |
| --- | --- | --- | --- | --- |
| | HARMONY | PRODUCTION | CONNECTION | STATUS QUO |
| COOPERATIVE (Positive Behavior) | Caring<br>Sensitive<br>Nurturing<br>Harmonizing<br>Feeling-oriented | Logical<br>Structured<br>Organized<br>Systematic<br>Thinking-oriented | Spontaneous<br>Creative<br>Playful<br>Enthusiastic<br>Action-oriented | Quiet<br>Imaginative<br>Insightful<br>Reflective<br>Inaction-oriented |
| RELUCTANT (Negative Behavior) | Overadaptive<br>Overpleasing<br>Makes mistakes<br>Cries or giggles<br>Self-defeating | Overcritical<br>Overworks<br>Perfectionist<br>Verbally attacks<br>Demanding | Disruptive<br>Blames<br>Irresponsible<br>Demands attention<br>Defiant | Disengaging<br>Withdrawn<br>Delays<br>Despondent<br>Daydreams |
| PSYCHOLOGICAL NEEDS | Friendships<br>Sensory experience | Task completion<br>Time schedule | Contact with people<br>Fun activities | Alone time<br>Stability |
| WAYS TO MEET NEEDS | Value their feelings<br>Comfortable work place<br>Pleasing learning environment<br>Cozy corner<br>Work with a friend | Value their ideas<br>Incentives<br>Rewards<br>Leadership positions<br>Schedules<br>To-do lists | Value their activity<br>Hands-on activities<br>Group interaction<br>Games<br>Change in routine | Value their privacy<br>Alone time<br>Independent activities<br>Specific directions<br>Computer activities<br>Routine tasks |

### Student Needs

When you understand the behaviors and needs that drive each personality type, you can provide a variety of choices in your classroom that allow these needs to be met. When your students' needs are met, they will most likely respond with cooperative behaviors.

In a classroom setting it works best to address all the students' needs in the classroom in a more global fashion by providing students a broad range of experiences, activities and interactions. Remember, students can learn the same content in many ways. Carefully plan your week to alternate between direct teaching, group activities, paired work and independent activities. Include higher level processing activities, relaxing activities and upbeat activities that provide physical stimulation. By providing a variety in your instructional strategies and presentations throughout the day, the students will more likely stay in cooperative, positive behaviors. The following student scenarios provide examples.

### Student Scenarios

**Harmony -** Shanel is primarily Harmony. Most of the time she is sensitive and caring. Friends are important to her, and she often praises her friends or shares kind notes of love and kindness. She feels for other people and wants everyone to like her. She provides support for someone who is feeling badly.

When Shanel is in a Reluctant mode of interaction, she tends to overadapt, overplease and make mistakes on the most simple items. This often leads to a loss of self-confidence. She wants to please others so much that she loses sight of her own goals. She also sometimes shows an attitude of helplessness, wanting to be "rescued." As Shanel's teacher, you can encourage Cooperative behavior by addressing her areas of need.

| Value Special Attributes | Provide Sensory Experiences |
|---|---|
| Use comments like, "I appreciate the way you make everyone in the class feel welcomed." | Create a comfortable working environment |
| Write a note on your stationary, letting her know you are glad she is in your class | Allow water bottles or snacks, as appropriate |
| Ask to assist with another student who has been absent | Work with a friend |

*What statement would be most encouraging for Shanel?*
a. Thank you for the way you are working.
b. Wow! Fantastic work!
c. You are such a caring person.

Answer: c.

**Production** - Marcus exhibits the Production personal objective strengths of being logical, structured, organized and persistent. He is a thinker, a problem solver, likes information exchange and values such things as task completion, skill development, and schedules. He is full of ideas and likes to share these with you and the class. He thrives on competition and enjoys seeing his work displayed. He likes printouts and postings showing his progress and achievement. He is efficient and his approach to assignments is always organized. He wants to know the plan for the hour.

When Marcus is stressed and moves into negative behaviors, he can become bossy or critical of himself and others. He may make fun of his friends' attempt at completing a task. He may put undue pressure on himself to do things perfectly and perceives that others are "having fun" while he is the only one working and being "responsible."

As Marcus' teacher, you can encourage him into Cooperative behavior by addressing his areas of need.

| Acknowledge Accomplishment and Work | Provide Time Schedule |
|---|---|
| Use tangible rewards, like presenting or sharing work with class | Start and end class on time |
| Verbally acknowledge skills | Be organized and prepared for class |
| Value thinking by asking for input | Have schedule of the day/period posted on board |
| Provide leadership position or job | Have routines |
| Meet with administrator to share class project | Announce changes in schedule |

*What statement would be most encouraging for Marcus?*
  a. I like your thinking.
  b. You make me happy.
  c. You're doing terrific.

Answer: a.

103

**Connection** - Rosario is operating from the Connection personal objective. He loves activity and action and comes into a room with a bounce. He is friendly and bright eyed. He connects with others in positive ways and enjoys being the center of attention. He likes loud music and drama, enjoys a good joke and likes to do things on the spur of the moment. He is full of ideas and very creative. He often asks his teacher, "Could we do it 'this' way instead?" He unconsciously taps his pencil and makes clicking noises with his tongue when he's working.

When in a Reluctant mode, Rosario can be disruptive, annoying, and attention-seeking. When he does "get in trouble," he blames others. Nothing is ever his fault; either the neighbor girl did it, the dog ate it or the rain made it too loud to hear the instructions. His pencil tapping becomes loud and intentional. His jokes become cruel, and he hurts other's feelings.

As Rosario's teacher, you can best encourage him to become Cooperative by addressing his areas of need.

| Provide Contact with Other People or the Environment | Have Fun |
|---|---|
| Use Think-Pair-Share | Include learning games |
| Engage in group activity | Offer a variety of activities |
| Write answers on individual chalkboards | Have activity ready at start of hour |
| Use manipulatives | Allow class presentations in front of class |
| Run errands | Consider unique or alternative ways to meet objectives |
| Chair upcoming class social | Allow for physical activity |

*What statement would be most encouraging for Rosario?*
a. You must be proud of the way you are working your mind.
b. Thumbs up on that one!
c. I appreciate the way you take pride in your work.

Answer: b.

**Status Quo -** Kylie shows the Status Quo personal objective. She is very quiet and shows little expression. She doesn't volunteer answers but when asked to contribute, she is exceptionally insightful. She prefers to work alone, enjoys working on the computer and is excellent at complex games. Kylie loves sustained, silent reading when she can sit quietly in the class or library and delve into a good book.

When Kylie becomes stressed, she withdraws. As she disengages from the learning experiences, she may exhibit a blank stare. She has trouble completing tasks, especially when the learning opportunities are more diverse and open-ended. Unfortunately, she may go unnoticed because she so quietly withdraws, sometimes to a point of despondency.

As Kylie's teacher, you can best encourage her into Cooperative behavior by addressing her areas of need.

| Provide Alone Time and/or Space | Provide Stability and Clear Directions |
| --- | --- |
| Engage in independent activity | Have set routines |
| Reflect with journal writing | Give clear step-by-step directions |
| Allow private time in classroom | Check progress frequently |

*What statement would be most encouraging for Kylie?*
a. I like your smile.
b. Thank you for the way you are working.
c. Wow! Fantastic work!

Answer: b.

105

**KNOW YOURSELF**

## ARRAY INTERACTION INVENTORY

Complete the following survey to help identify your primary and secondary personal objectives, the most natural ways you tend to respond to the world.

Directions:

- Rank order the responses in rows below on a scale from 1 to 4 with

    **1 being "least like me"** to **4 being "most like me."**

- After you have ranked each row, add down each column.

- The column/s with the highest score/s shows your primary Personal Objective/s.

| In your normal day-to-day life, you tend to be: | | | | | | | |
|---|---|---|---|---|---|---|---|
| Nurturing Sensitive Caring | | Logical Systematic Organized | | Spontaneous Creative Playful | | Quiet Insightful Reflective | |

| In your normal day-to-day life, you tend to value: | | | | | | | |
|---|---|---|---|---|---|---|---|
| Harmony Relationships | | Work Time schedules | | Stimulation Having fun | | Reflection Having some time alone | |

| In most settings, you are usually: | | | | | | | |
|---|---|---|---|---|---|---|---|
| Authentic Compassionate Harmonious | | Traditional Responsible Parental | | Active Opportunistic Spontaneous | | Inventive Competent Seeking | |

| In most situations, you could be described as: | | | | | | | |
|---|---|---|---|---|---|---|---|
| Empathetic Communicative Devoted | | Practical Competitive Loyal | | Impetuous Impactful Daring | | Conceptual Knowledgeable Composed | |

| You approach most tasks in a(n) _____ manner. | | | | | | | |
|---|---|---|---|---|---|---|---|
| Affectionate Inspirational Vivacious | | Conventional Orderly Concerned | | Courageous Adventurous Impulsive | | Rational Philosophical Complex | |

| When things start to "not go your way" and you are tired and worn down, what might your responses be? | | | | | | | |
|---|---|---|---|---|---|---|---|
| Say "I'm sorry" Make mistakes Feel badly | | Overcontrol Become critical Take charge | | "It's not my fault" Manipulate Act out | | Withdraw Not talk Become indecisive | |

| When you've "had a bad day" and you become frustrated, how might you respond? | | | | | | | |
|---|---|---|---|---|---|---|---|
| Overplease Cry Feel depressed | | Be perfectionistic Verbally attack Overwork | | Become physical Be irresponsible Demand attention | | Disengage Delay Daydream | |

| Add score: | | | | | | | |
|---|---|---|---|---|---|---|---|
| **Harmony** | | **Production** | | **Connection** | | **Status Quo** | |

©Kortman, 1997

**KNOW YOUR MANAGEMENT/INSTRUCTIONAL STYLE**

Knowing your own primary personality/personal objectives will also help you better understand the type of management/instructional style that is most natural for you. Your plan to include varying styles will help accommodate the diverse learning styles of your students. There are four basic management/instructional styles that compliment the four personal objectives.

**Inclusive -** The teacher fosters a sense of belonging by interacting in a nurturing and accepting way, valuing students' feelings and developing a community of learners in a safe and secure environment. (Accentuates *Harmony* favored learning style.)

Example: "I appreciate the way you give ideas and work together with your group. The plants I brought today will help us understand how important their existence is for our ability to live on the earth."

**Informational -** The teacher encourages group participation and decision-making. There is interaction between teacher and students that is focused on gathering and processing information. (Supports *Production* favored learning style.)

Example: "Today we are going to study the plant life in our region. Will you please turn to page 24 in your text? Let's discuss question number one together."

**Interactive -** The teacher invites students to assume as much responsibility as they can handle. Students are encouraged to interact creatively with what is being learned. (Assists *Connection* favored learning style.)

Example: "Let's learn about plants today. What are some projects or assignments we can generate to help us learn about the plants in our state?"

**Independent -** The teacher gives clear, concise directives; the teacher tells the students what to do and how to do it, then allows them to work independently. (Appeals to *Status Quo* favored learning style.)

Example: "Take out your science text, turn to page 24 and answer the first five questions in your journal."

The most effective teachers use all four styles at various times in their classrooms. It is important for you to capitalize on your style/s of strength; however keep in mind that a majority of students respond best to a higher concentration of the Informational and Inclusive styles.

## KNOW WHERE YOUR MANAGEMENT PHILOSOPHY "FITS"

The Discipline/Management Continuum presents the major discipline models/ philosophies and their underlying practices that are currently being used in schools throughout the United States. Knowing where you currently fit along this spectrum will help you describe your practice to students, parents, colleagues and administrators. As you continue to teach, you may find that you create your own approach by combining the best fit from various models.

### The Discipline/Management Continuum

Behavioristic
Corrective control
Teacher directed

Humanistic
Proactive measures
Student directed

←————————————————————————————————————→

| Behavior Analysis (Skinner) | Assertive Discipline (Canter) | Positive Discipline Model (Jones) | Social Discipline Model (Dreikurs) | Array Management Model (Kortman) | Choice Theory (Glasser) | Teacher Effectiveness (Gordon) |

|  | DESCRIPTION: | ROLE OF TEACHER: | IMPLEMENTATION: | EMPHASIS: |
|---|---|---|---|---|
| Behavior Analysis (derived from learning theory of Skinner) | Observable behavior is changed by the systematic application of behavior modification techniques. | Arrange consequences and control conditions to reinforce good behavior and punish bad behavior. | Target the behavior for change, shape, model and use reinforcers and punishment. | The behavior is treated as the problem, not as a symptom of a problem. |
| Assertive Discipline (Canter) | Assertiveness training is applied with verbal assertiveness and rewards and punishments. | Assertively insist that students behave properly and follow through with a well-organized procedure when they do not behave. | Establish a discipline plan with specified rules and use a check system with a hierarchy of teacher-supplied consequences to match student behavior. | Deal with the misbehavior quickly and return to teaching objectives, giving strength to corrective control. |
| Positive Discipline Model (Jones) | With the goal of increasing student engagement time and decreasing lost instructional time, an incentive process is utilized to help students support their own self-control and be influenced by peer pressure. | Provide a structured classroom and use body language, incentive systems and individual assistance. | Use limit setting, responsibility training, back-up systems and omission training within an incentive program. | Increase time on-task in the classroom. |

Behavioristic
Corrective control
Teacher directed

Humanistic
Proactive measures
Student directed

←――――――――――――――――――――――――――――――――――→

| Behavior Analysis (Skinner) | Assertive Discipline (Canter) | Positive Discipline Model (Jones) | Social Discipline Model (Dreikurs) | Array Management Model (Kortman) | Choice Theory (Glasser) | Teacher Effectiveness (Gordon) |

|  | DESCRIPTION: | ROLE OF TEACHER: | IMPLEMENTATION: | EMPHASIS: |
|---|---|---|---|---|
| Social Discipline Model (Dreikurs) | Emphasis is on equality, respect, cooperation, self-discipline and encouragement. People are capable of changing and human problems are interpersonal and socially embedded. | Provide a relationship with the students based on trust and respect and identify one of four mistaken goals exhibited by a child when a problem arises and respond accordingly. | Offer democratic classroom where students help determine rules and suffer the logical consequences of their own misbehaviors. | In a preventive and supportive way, meet the students' needs to belong in the dynamic of a class group seen as a social entity. |
| Array Management Model (Kortman) | Components of self-management and encouragement are incorporated in this model that focuses on situational variables and internal motivators that influence individual choices. | Orchestrate the class by providing a variety of choices in learning and interacting in an atmosphere that capitalizes on individual strengths and interaction styles. | Use proactive strategies for inviting all students to function in a cooperative mode. Consequences and identifying replacement behaviors are key components to corrective management. | Each person is self-disciplined. Teacher and students are encouraged to remain in positive and productive behavior, capitalizing on strengths in interacting and learning. |
| Choice Theory (Glasser) | Quality work of the students is the focal point for a preventive management strategy. | Be a lead manager who stimulates, provides help to students, demonstrates ways work can be done, emphasizes student evaluation of their own work. | Provide an environment to help students make good choices about quality work, have class meetings individual plans to redirect students when misbehavior occurs. | School needs to be a good place. Focus on skills that apply to life and the use of problem solving as the basis for making good choices. |
| Teacher Effectiveness Training (Gordon) | Self-concept and emotional development are the basis for this communication based model, which uses active listening, I-messages and conflict resolution. | Supportive and noncritical facilitator helps students identify and solve their own problems, emphasizing the relationship between the students and teacher. | Identify areas for acceptable and unacceptable behaviors, give ownership to who owns the problem and utilize strategies for each possibility. | Students control their own behavior through problem solving and the teacher is a facilitator for growth. |

# Notes:

# BUILDING MANAGEMENT FOR THE ELEMENTARY YEARS

The previous section has outlined many proactive measures and strategies. This section will provide specific elementary school examples of proactive strategies and address the implementation of supportive and corrective measures. Working examples for utilizing positive reinforcement statements, developing rules and consequences, a responsibility plan, and a checklist for a discipline challenge will also be provided.

## PROACTIVE MEASURES

It is your job as the teacher to set a tone of positive and encouraging interactions in your classroom. Your tone and demeanor basically determine how the students will respond to you. Teachers should also develop clear expectations and provide multiple opportunities for students to succeed. One way to facilitate student success is by always highlighting behavior that is appropriate and desired. Since it takes a person four to seven times longer to process negative information than positive, keeping your comments focused on what you want to occur helps with communication and response time.

### *Use Positive Phrasing*

Encouragement is the key to building on student strengths. Following are examples of positive phrases that encourage students. Remember, positive phrases help students know what to do, while negative phrases are often confusing.

- ❖ "I appreciate the way Kristen is listening."
- ❖ "Taylor is ready to begin."
- ❖ "I am looking for eyes on me. Thank you, Jordan. Thank you, Maria."
- ❖ "I appreciate all the diligent workers I see."
- ❖ "You are really concentrating. Thank you."
- ❖ "There are many good thinkers in this room."

Other positive verbal cues include statements such as:

- ❖ "If you're listening to me, look at me and smile."
- ❖ "If you're ready for instructions, pick up your pencil."
- ❖ "If you're ready to begin, fold your hands."

### *Positive Reinforcement Statements*

Positive statements help produce an atmosphere that is uplifting and encouraging. When using positive statements with students, remember that the students are different in what they value as important. Some enjoy hearing how good they are at their work, others appreciate hearing that the teacher just enjoys having them in the class and others are motivated by your enthusiasm. Although the positive reinforcement statements give you a starting point, remember that the most beneficial feedback is specific. Highlight specific aspects of academic work or specific behaviors for reinforcement.

*"Keep up the great work!"*

### Positive Reinforcement Statements

* Thank you for the way you are listening.

* Thank you for the way you are working.

* You are right with me.

* You are thinking.

* That's the way to do it.

* You are doing first class work.

* I bet you're proud of the way you're working.

* You are creating wonderful masterpieces.

* I like the way you are working your minds.

* You should feel good about your efforts.

* Wow! Fantastic work!

* Keep up the great work.

* You're doing beautifully.

* I can tell you take pride in your work.

* You are fabulous.

* You are showing great brainpower.

* You bring a wonderful feeling to our class.

* Thumbs up on that one!

* I like your smile.

113

### *Gain and Keep Student Attention*

Gaining and keeping the attention of your students is critical to the smooth management of your class. Auditory cues are most effective for gaining attention because they allow students to remain actively engaged in an activity or assignment until they hear something that signals them to listen and prepares them for a change of routine or activities. Some effective approaches include using positive reinforcement phrasing, chimes, a rain stick, clapping, a music box, listening/writing cues or whispering.

 Variety in your positive approaches eliminates boredom in responding to the same cue each time, so gradually build up an array of approaches to use throughout the day as you need the students' attention.

The following examples provide effective ways for teachers to gain and keep the attention of students.

**Take Five -** With this approach the teacher holds up five fingers on one hand and says, "Take Five." The students have been taught what five things they are expected to initiate when they hear and see that cue. For example: 1) Desk clear, 2) Seated at desk, 3) Hands in lap, 4) Mouth quiet, and 5) Eyes on teacher. The teacher can then continue by slowly counting down from 5 to 1, with everyone ready by 1.

**Rhythmic Clapping -** The teacher can use clapping patterns to gain attention and signal response back from the students. The teacher claps a pattern and the students mimic the same pattern. This is continued until the majority of the class has joined in.

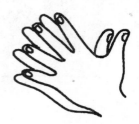

**Music Box -** This technique encourages quick listening response and attention. Wind up the music box at the beginning of the week. When you play the music, the students know to be quiet and ready. When all the students are ready, shut the lid. At the end of the week, if there is any music left to be played, the students receive a pre-determined bonus, like a improvisational time or quiet ball.

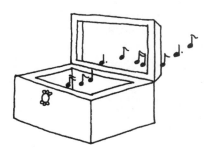

**Writing Cue -** An example of a writing cue is: "If you're listening to me, you will put the name of your favorite breakfast cereal on the bottom left side of your paper." Every day change what you have the students put on the paper and where you have them place it. It becomes a game for them to listen. Be creative. It can be as simple as a smiling face or it can be reinforcement for something just learned. For example, "List five of the seven continents on the upper right-hand corner of your paper."

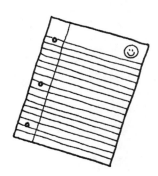

**Rain Stick -** A rain stick can be hand-made or purchased at a nature store and has a soft, soothing tone that encourages a positive response in students of all ages. To make one of your own, see the following page.

**Rain Stick Directions**

**Materials:**

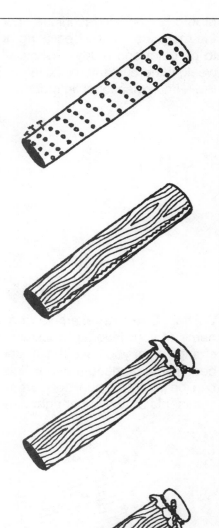

- wrapping paper tube
- 120 small straight sewing pins
- wood grain contact paper
- material scraps or suede squares
  (to cover ends of the rain stick)
- heavy-duty cord
  (to tie materials or suede to the ends)
- ½ cup dried rice
- ¼ cup dried lentils
- ¼ cup dried beans

**Directions:**

1. Poke all 120 pins into the wrapping paper tube in a circular pattern. Make sure to stick the pin all the way through the tube. (You will leave these pins because they produce the "thinking" sound of the rain stick.)

2. Cover the tube and all of the ends of the pins with the contact paper.

3. Cover one end with the material or suede.

4. Fill tube with dry ingredients.

5. Cover the other end with your material and tie off to finish.

Enjoy your rain stick!

### *Encourage Student Engagement*

Keeping your students actively involved facilitates learning and actually makes classroom management easier. The following suggestions are easy ways to keep students involved.

**Question and Response Techniques** - Help students keep their minds engaged and actively involved in the lesson.

❖ Ask question first, then call on a student to respond.

❖ Give sufficient "wait time" for students to process their thinking before calling on someone for a response.

❖ Ask follow-up questions. Why? Can you tell me more? Give us an example.

❖ Ask clarifying questions. Can you tell us how you got your answer?

❖ Have students develop their own questions.

❖ Have a student give a summary of what has been learned in a lesson.

❖ Have methods for every student to participate. For instance:

   o Thumbs up or down.
   o Yes/No cards.
   o Individual chalkboards or dry erase boards.
   o Have students pair with one other student to give response.

**Think-Pair-Share** - Give the students something to think about individually. Then allow them to share their thinking with a neighbor. Then have a few students share with the whole class.

**Variety** - New approaches and activities always excite and interest students. Some examples include:

❖ Provide variety in individual, partner and group activities.

❖ Use manipulatives.

❖ Use alternative learning methods: plays, presentations and/or games.

❖ Have groups of students teach various sections from a chapter or text. Let them do added research and determine methods of presentation.

117

### *Be Prepared*

Keeping students engaged also means the teacher is prepared. The following list offers ideas for initiating your success.

| What To Do | How To Do It |
| --- | --- |
| Set clear expectations. | Have 2 or 3 guidelines for behavior. |
| Provide engaging lessons that encourage active participation. | Use games, activity cards, whiteboards for multiple responses. |
| Utilize effective organization skills. | Be prepared with all paperwork before class time. |
| Establish and maintain routines. | Have students fulfill job responsibilities. |
| Effectively focus and retain student's and group attention. | Use multiple strategies. Have a good set. Have relevant activities. Adjust to age-appropriate attention span. |
| Provide clear instruction. | Plan. Plan. Plan. |
| Build positive relationships. | Relate to students in their areas of interest. |
| Provide relevant learning choices. | Focus on process of learning, not just product. |
| Understand and adapt to student needs. | Use a variety of learning strategies. |

 Videotape yourself teaching a lesson. Observe your interaction with the students carefully. Use the "What to Do" and "How to Do It" lists as your observation guide.

## UTILIZE SUPPORTIVE AND CORRECTIVE BACK-UP STRATEGIES

Proactive measures are used to prevent and minimize management challenges and set your students up for success in the classroom. Being attentive to your students, moving among them, providing feedback continuously, and reinforcing signs of positive behavior allow you to immediately accommodate student needs before they spiral into negative behavior. When you first sense students slipping into Marginal behavior, supportive measures allow you to give them a choice to come back into positive behavior. When students choose nonproductive behaviors despite your proactive and supportive attempts, it's time to step in with corrective measures. It is critical to set up a code of conduct with consequences so the students know what to expect when they make choices to do something inappropriate. To be effective, you must be consistent in your delivery and response, yet flexible as you adjust to student differences.

### *Understand and Adjust to Student Differences*

Positive reinforcement for one student can be perceived as a negative consequence for another. Have logical and natural consequences that match motivations for differing students. The chart below offers examples of possible reinforcements and one consequence that would capitalize on each student's dominant, personal objective.

### Reinforcement and Consequence Chart

|  | HARMONY | PRODUCTION | CONNECTION | STATUS QUO |
|---|---|---|---|---|
| **Positive Reinforcement** | Work with friends<br><br>Have stuffed animal | Receive award<br><br>Post papers | Play a game<br><br>Work with friends | Have alone time<br><br>Work independently on computer |
| **Consequences** | Verbal redirection | Written contract | Loss of privilege | Behavior log |

 Check yourself: "Students, don't talk" vs. "Students, please be quiet." Videotape yourself. How often do you give students negative directives? How often do you offer affirmative guidance? Affirmative guidance actually shapes students' behavior more quickly.

### *Provide Logical and Natural Consequences*

The most effective guidelines or rules for the classroom encompass many concepts and behaviors in one positively stated phrase. As you discuss positively stated phrases, you are actually teaching your students.

> *Example:* "Show respect to all people and property."

Use logical consequences as your predominant corrective tool when students violate rules. You will see more sustained progress for appropriate and desired behavior choices. The initial investment will be well worth it!

**Natural Consequence** - An outcome students experience as a natural result of their behavior.

> *Example*: Adam blurts out answers.

> **Natural consequence** - Other students become annoyed at Adam.

**Logical Consequence** - An outcome arranged by someone that is directly associated with the negative behavior choice.

> *Example*: Adam blurts out answers.

> **Logical consequence -** Teacher calls on a student with hand raised and does not acknowledge Adam's comment.

***Using natural and logical consequences keeps students enthusiastic.***

**Behaviors and Consequences -** Think about the things that make sense for differing personality components/personal objectives. Two students may look at the same consequence, staying in at recess, very differently. Someone primary in Status Quo might look at this as a reward, while someone primary in Connection would consider it a definite punishment.

Write a consequence for each student behavior listed below. Think of appropriate consequences that are natural or logical. Think about the Personal Objectives (PO) of students who would exhibit various behaviors. Attempt to provide consequences that match student's Personal Objectives.

*Example:* Robbie (P.O. Connection) yells out answers without raising hand.
*Logical consequence:* Call on a student with hand raised without acknowledging Robbie's response.

Student's P.O. : Harmony
Problem: Talking with neighbor.
Logical Consequences:

Student's P.O. : Connection
Problem: Giggling and laughing during class discussion.
Logical Consequences:

Student's P.O. : Status Quo
Problem: Not answering when called upon.
Logical Consequences:

Student's P.O. : Production
Problem: Telling others how incompetent they are.
Logical Consequences:

121

## Rules and Consequences

List your **CLASSROOM RULES OR GUIDELINES** (No more than five).

*Example: Show respect to all people and property.*

Give your **RULE RATIONALE**.

*Example: Great opportunity to teach students about respect. Guideline is broad enough to cover most classroom behavior choices.*

List the **CONSEQUENCES** for breaking a rule.

*Examples: a. Talk with teacher, b. Write behavior contract with commitment for change and agreed upon choice of consequence, c. Reinforce positive change.*
   *\*Do the consequences match the misbehavior?
   *\*Do the consequences make sense for differing Personal Objectives?

**TEACHER SELF-CHECK**

How will I enforce rules?
   *Examples: Model respect. Give positive verbal feedback identifying students showing respect to teacher and other students. Follow through consistently with reinforcements and consequences.*

How will I follow through?
   *Example: When respect is not shown, a logical consequence will be issued.*

How will I help students be responsible for their own behavior?
   *Examples: Make expectations clear. Talk through scenarios with students. Give positive reasons for choosing appropriate behavior. Set up behavior contract form and have it ready for use. Give students opportunities to redirect their behavior.*

How will I encourage positive behaviors?
   *Example: Provide verbal reinforcement for those showing respect and specifically label their behavior. "I appreciate the way Laura showed respect to Jason by looking at him while he was responding to the question."*

# Rules and Consequences Template

| CLASSROOM RULES OR GUIDELINES |
|---|
| 1. |
| 2. |
| 3. |
| 4. |
| 5. |

| RULE RATIONALE |
|---|
| 1. |
| 2. |
| 3. |
| 4. |
| 5. |

| CONSEQUENCES |
|---|
| 1. |
| 2. |
| 3. |
| 4. |
| 5. |

| TEACHER SELF-CHECK |
|---|
| How will I enforce rules? |
| How will I follow through? |
| How will I help students be responsible for their own behavior? |
| How will I encourage positive behaviors? |

## Responsibility Plan

My name is _____

| The rule I broke: |
| --- |
| |
| My consequence: |
| |
| |

| My plan for change: |
| --- |
| |
| |

**I can make responsible choices in the classroom.  I will choose to control myself and help make this a productive place for myself and all the other students.**

Student signature _____

Teacher signature _____

Date _____

Follow-Up _____

### *Underlying Problems May Not Be School Related*

Unfortunately, there are times when a student will continue to be disruptive or non-productive no matter what you do to make the lesson engaging, the activity relevant and the visual aids compelling. Sometimes a student has developed a failure pattern that is very difficult to modify or change. Realize that the key for changing this behavior is consistency over time. Try your best to understand this student. Find consistent ways to reinforce positive behavior and set up consistent procedures to hold this student accountable for their negative behavior choices. Your positive persistence will eventually give you and the student a chance to celebrate the positive changes.

The following steps are effective for any student:

1. Respect and value students.
2. Develop and teach clear expectations.
3. Provide choices in learning and interacting.
4. Model positive behavior.
5. Reinforce positive behavior.
6. Consistently and calmly follow through with consequences.

### *Ask the Students!*

When in doubt, initiate dialogue and let you students talk to you. Students will often give you cues for what they need to maintain positive behavior. These personalized interactions can often be the catalyst for significant changes in behavior. Use this time to create a behavior contract with the student. Putting a responsibility plan into writing provides important motivation for a change in behavior by providing accountability for misbehavior, identification of replacement behaviors, a plan for redirecting behavior and an emphasis on reinforcing positive behaviors. It also provides documentation for your records.

### *Checklist for a Challenge*

The following checklist provides basic questions to guide you through a plan of action for developing clear expectations and consistent, logical consequences that are appropriate for each student. It also guides your reflections as you consider the interactions between student motivation and teacher behaviors.

## Checklist for a Challenge

| PLAN OF ACTION |
| --- |

1. What is the plan of action for the student?

2. Does the student know what to expect?

3. What are the steps to take?

4. What are the consequences for inappropriate behavior choices?

5. How will I follow through?

| SELF-CHECK | Yes | No |
| --- | --- | --- |
| 1. Am I consistent in my methods for follow-through? | ☐ | ☐ |
| 2. Was I well prepared for the class period and lesson? | ☐ | ☐ |
| 3. Did I have materials organized and ready for student use? | ☐ | ☐ |
| 4. Did I portray enthusiasm in my teaching? | ☐ | ☐ |
| 5. Did I provide a variety of activities? | ☐ | ☐ |
| 6. Did I have clear expectations? What were they? | ☐ | ☐ |
| 7. Did I provide clear directions? What were they? | ☐ | ☐ |

| STUDENT CHECK |
| --- |

1. Is this a first time problem for the student or a pattern of behavior?

2. What other factors may have impacted the student's choice for negative behavior?

3. Does there seem to be corresponding problems in the area of academics?

4. Does there seem to be corresponding problems in the area of social interactions?

5. Does there seem to be corresponding problems from the home environment?

### The Student Is Not His Actions

When a student has behaved inappropriately, separate the action from the student. Let the student know what specific behavior was unacceptable; help identify appropriate behaviors, then give the student an opportunity to make a change. Let the student know you believe in their ability to make good choices in the future.

*Trade Secrets*

## CHAPTER CHECKLIST

As you review your classroom management system you will need to reflect upon a number of interrelated concerns. Ask yourself, do I:

Yes   No

☐ ☐ Build positive relationships with all students?
☐ ☐ Model positive attitudes, behaviors and interactions?
☐ ☐ Encourage positive interactions from and among students?
☐ ☐ Reinforce positive behavior on a continual basis?

☐ ☐ Set clear expectations?
☐ ☐ Establish meaningful routines?
☐ ☐ Have all materials ready before class begins?
☐ ☐ Use clear auditory cues for focusing and keeping group attention?
☐ ☐ Use positive phrasing?
☐ ☐ Provide engaging lessons?
☐ ☐ Include all students in class activities?
☐ ☐ Provide clear instructions for work and assignments?

☐ ☐ Provide multiple opportunities for students to succeed?
☐ ☐ Provide relevant learning choices?
☐ ☐ Focus on the process of learning?
☐ ☐ Understand varying Personal Objectives and their motivation for work and behavior?
☐ ☐ Have a variety in each day to provide for varying Personal Objectives/ personality components?
Ex: - independent, paired and group work, hands-on activities, games
     - journal writing, reading, worksheets, review, higher order thinking
☐ ☐ Understand Cooperative, Marginal and Reluctant modes of interaction?
☐ ☐ Understand and adapt to student needs?
☐ ☐ Value/respect students for who they are?
☐ ☐ Provide sensory experiences?
☐ ☐ Value work and accomplishments of students?
☐ ☐ Give students a time schedule for the day's events?
☐ ☐ Provide opportunities for contact with other students and materials?
☐ ☐ Have fun, unique and creative activities and assignments?
☐ ☐ Allow for independent work?
☐ ☐ Provide specific directions?

| Yes | No | |
|---|---|---|
| ☐ | ☐ | Know my preferred Management/Instructional Style? - Independent, Informational, Inclusive, Interactive |
| ☐ | ☐ | Incorporate all four styles into my teaching? |
| ☐ | ☐ | Know what management philosophy fits best for me? |
| ☐ | ☐ | Know how I will implement my management philosophy? |
| ☐ | ☐ | Adjust consequences to meet students' needs? |
| ☐ | ☐ | Consistently and calmly follow through with consequences? |
| ☐ | ☐ | Utilize logical and natural consequences for inappropriate behavior choices? |
| ☐ | ☐ | Ask the students what they need and talk to them at their level? |
| ☐ | ☐ | Solicit feedback from students about my teaching and their learning? |
| ☐ | ☐ | Separate the student's actions from the student? |
| ☐ | ☐ | Recognize that some problems are unrelated to school? |

## Notes:

# Chapter 4

# COMMUNICATING WITH PARENTS

**Section A:**   **Open House - Meet the Teacher**
- ❖ Encouraging Attendance
- ❖ Open House Presentation
    - o Activities
    - o Reviewing Teaching Approach
    - o Contact Form
    - o Room Roam

**Section B:**   **Classroom Publications**
- ❖ Weekly Newsletters
- ❖ Monthly Newsletters
- ❖ News Flashes

**Section C:**   **Personal Interactions**
- ❖ Phone Calls and Emails
- ❖ Problem-Solving Interactions

**Chapter Checklist**

An important aspect of building community is establishing positive rapport with parents. One of a teacher's most important tasks is to communicate with the parents about their students. Research consistently reveals that when parents are involved in their son/daughter's education, the student, of any age, benefits. Teachers who effectively and frequently communicate with parents increase the chances that parents will:

- ❖ Become meaningfully involved in their son/daughter's education.
- ❖ Reinforce classroom instruction.
- ❖ Support the teacher's management system.

*Parents should always feel welcome.*

Chapter 2 offered several suggestions about how to establish communication with parents prior to the start of school. This chapter discussed effective ongoing ways to communicate with parents via personal contact and informal instructional publications. Chapter 5 provides information about sharing student progress with parents.

**Section A**

## OPEN HOUSE — MEET THE TEACHER

Meeting parents at Open House or Meet the Teacher Night is exciting. The opportunity to meet parents personally is a great chance to expand your knowledge of your students and describe your instructional program. To encourage attendance, it is important to formally invite parents early and remind them frequently of the day and time of the Open House.

**Open House Invitation**

ANYTOWN SCHOOLS

Welcomes Your Family
to
Open House
Tuesday, September 12
Classroom Presentation Times:

Kindergarten 7:00 p.m.  First Grade 7:20 p.m.
Second Grade 7:40 p.m.  Third Grade 8:00 p.m.
Fourth Grade 8:20 p.m.  Fifth Grade 8:40 p.m.

Student entertainment, Door prizes, Refreshments
See You There!

### ENCOURAGING ATTENDANCE

Experienced teachers and administrators have found parental attendance increases when you:

❖ Welcome the entire family. Baby-sitters may be hard to find and are usually expensive.

❖ Organize student presentations in your classroom. This may require coordination with other grade level/subject areas.

❖ Serve light refreshments. Ask for parent contributions or ask the parent organization.

❖ Hold drawings for door prizes, e.g., children's books, markers, fancy pencils or items with the school logo.

133

## OPEN HOUSE PRESENTATION

### *Activities*

Successful open houses also allow teachers to inform parents about the learning activities their children are experiencing. Listed below are several other activities that can be organized for open house.

**Volunteer Cards** - Have parents fill out a volunteer card. Volunteer cards help teachers know which types of activities parents would be willing to assist with. Cards can also be used for drawing door prizes.

**Class Quilt** - Students and the teacher draw and label pictures of themselves. Arrange pictures in a quilt fashion. This creates a strong sense of classroom community.

*A classroom quilt is a great way to demonstrate a sense of community.*

**Parent Notes and Name Tags** - All students make their parents' name tags, then write a welcome note to their family, and place it on their desks or tables.

**Teacher Presentation** - Dress professionally and SMILE. This presentation should be brief, positive and enthusiastic. Address issues such as daily schedules, classroom rules and expectations, learning centers, homework assignments and special activities.

**Handouts** - Provide a handout that summarizes the content of the presentation. Remember, the handout may need to be translated into other languages.

**Students' Show** - A 10-minute presentation can be a wonderful way to highlight the students' contributions. Students can do group songs, finger plays and/or choral poems.

**Learning Centers** - Label each learning center and provide a handout that describes how each center contributes to the students' education. Post two or three students at each center to discuss and demonstrate center activities (see pages 137-140).

**Volunteer Cards**

Parent Names _____

Student's Name _____

Home Phone _____

Work Phone _____

Email _____

### I would be willing to:

_____ Coordinate classroom parties

_____ Make learning center games
     ___ at home  ___ at school

_____ Work in classroom
_____ Tutor children
_____ Other

_____

_____

Please list any special talents you would be willing to share.

Open house is another time to encourage parents to become classroom volunteers (see Chapter 2 for more information).

## *Reviewing Teaching Approach*

There are many approaches to teaching. Parents appreciate knowing how and what their children will be taught this year in your classroom.

Many elementary teachers use a centers approach to instruction. To help parents understand the educational value of learning centers, you may wish to share briefly how you use the centers in your classroom. Parents usually want to know:

❖ How often do the children work/learn in centers?

❖ How long are they allowed to work/learn in centers?

❖ How does the teacher determine who works/learns in each center?
(Free choice, rotation)

❖ How does the teacher monitor the children's learning during center time?

❖ How do centers meet the individual needs of each student?

❖ What do the centers teach?

Provide a brief overview about the instructional approaches you will be using, for example, cooperative learning. Perhaps the most visible approach the parents will see at open house would be classroom organization that supports the learning environment.

The following pages provide an easy-to-understand "Guide to Learning Opportunities Through Centers." Elementary teachers may use or adapt this resource at open house.

**Language and Literacy Development**

Thematic Play
"Grocery Store"

Story Retelling

Thematic Play
"Café"

Dramatic play centers provide children an opportunity to: reveal thoughts and attitudes through conversations; use knowledge of print to enhance play; learn to share, plan, organize and take turns; and demonstrate understanding of the many functions of print.

**Language and Literacy Development**

Library Center

Writing Center

Listening Center

Language-related centers provide students with an opportunity to: enjoy good literature; practice language skills; increase vocabulary; learn how to handle books, tapes, CDs; listen to and tell stories; extend attention span; and share thoughts through writing.

**Numeracy, Spatial and Logical Thinking Development**

Math Center

Block Center

Science Center

Manipulative centers provide students an opportunity to: think, reason, problem-solve; experience concepts of size, shape, quantity and position; experience counting; understand part-to-whole; eye/hand coordination; examine and predict outcomes; and classify and categorize.

139

**Creative Development**

Music Center

Puppetry Center

Art Center

Expressive centers provide students the opportunity to: respond to music; create music; dance and sing; create stories, pictures, crafts; express emotional states; and appreciate the creative efforts of others.

## *Contact Form*

Open House is a night to meet and welcome all families. Unfortunately, some parents may try to monopolize your time to deal with more personal issues. If parents try to engage you in an individual conference, you can firmly and politely redirect them by offering a contact form to complete.

**Contact Form**

Student's Name _____ Parent Name/s _____

Home Phone _____ Work Phone _____

Do you wish to make a private appointment?   Yes _____   No _____

Best times for you to meet _____

Particular concerns _____

_____

Using the contact form allows you time to discuss the parents' concerns with appropriate school administration or staff.

❖ Wear a name tag and greet parents at the door.
❖ If you have need for volunteers, have parents fill out a volunteer card. See included form.
❖ Make sure you know where resource information is available, e.g., where to obtain a map, student schedule and/or questions about schedule changes.
❖ Check with front office for any universal message the administrative and/or department may want on the board for all parents to read, e.g., tardy policy.

## Room Roam

Some schools conduct a "Meet the Teacher" event just prior to the opening of school. If this is the case at your school, you will want to focus on learning more about the students. For example, you may wish to have parents complete the student information letter during this meeting (see pages 64 and 66).

During "Meet the Teacher," the parents and students can complete the "Room Roam" together. This fun activity allows the family to become familiar with the classroom.

---

*Room Roam*

1. Find your desk. It has your name on it.

2. Make nametags for you and your parents.

3. Find the fish tank.
   Count the number of fish in the fish tank.

4. Find the Birthday Chart.
   When is your birthday?
   Write it on the Birthday Chart.

5. Find the Tooth Graph.
   How many teeth have you lost?
   Put that number on the Tooth Graph.

6. Find the "Me" bulletin board.
   Draw your portrait and write your name on it.
   Then put it on the "Me" bulletin board.

7. Find the information desk. Have your parents complete the information forms in the "Back-to-School Kit."

8. Make a new friend.

---

**Section B**

## CLASSROOM PUBLICATIONS

Communicating with parents can be done most effectively if done proactively. Classroom publications should be designed to review student's learning activities or directly inform parents about specific concepts.

When you send home newsletters be sure to attach them to your lesson plans. This practice provides you a complete and immediate record of correspondence.

### WEEKLY NEWSLETTERS

One-page newsletters need to be sent weekly. They should:

❖ Be reader-friendly and conversational.

❖ Review briefly the high points of last week's learning.

❖ Preview the goals and activities planned for the coming week.

❖ Recognize parents who have helped to support classroom learning; for example, parents who accompanied the class on a field trip.

❖ Be sent home consistently on one particular day of the week; Mondays are generally best.

The following page offers an example of a weekly newsletter. Notice how Ms. Jones reviews the previous week's activities, taking the opportunity to thank parents who have provided supplies and/or support. Next, she describes the focus of this week's curriculum and provides suggestions to help parents reinforce this information at home. Notice how the teacher uses friendly, everyday language to introduce and explain new concepts.

English may not be the parents' first language. Therefore, a teacher should attempt to have all written communication translated into the language appropriate for the student's parents.

143

## *Weekly Newsletter Examples*

Dear Parents:

Last week we took a field trip to the hospital. Our trip was exciting and we learned even more about how doctors and nurses serve our community. Have your son/daughter read you the story they wrote and illustrated after our field trip. One of the most exciting stops in the hospital was the baby nursery. All of the children were interested in their own first stay at the hospital. Perhaps you will share your memories about that big event. Our class thanks Mrs. Delgado and Mrs. Ortiz for being chaperones. They also helped our students write their stories.

This week we will discuss fire safety at home and school. Our first lesson is called "Stop, Drop and Roll," teaching us what to do if our clothes catch on fire. We will also map a safe fire exit from our classroom and review appropriate behavior during an emergency. We will actually have a school-wide fire drill to practice these skills. Because you and your child's safety is so important, I am asking that you and your son/daughter draw a map of your house and design the best fire escape route. This home activity will reinforce the fire safety concepts the children are learning in school. On Friday we will go to our local fire station. (See attached permission slip.) Since this is a walking field trip, I will need at least four parent volunteers. I hope you can join us.

To help all of us learn more about fire safety, the Fire Marshall will provide the children and their families with a booklet called, "Learn Not To Burn." The book is available in Spanish. Please review this informative booklet with your son/daughter. If you have any personal experiences in the area of fire safety, please let me know. You can be an expert speaker for our classroom.

Sincerely,

Ms. Jones

Another way children can communicate with their parents is through a personal weekly summary letter. For example: Abby's note is written to her parents. It describes her view of her learning. Notice that Abby, a third grader, is using developmental spelling even at this time of the year. The letter is completed on a form that leaves space for the teacher to share her comments also.

# Fantastic Week!!

Dear Mom & Dad,

This week in March we did probability. We took a couple of time tests too. Also we learned about counting change. It was fun.

In reading we read Mrs. Piggle Wiggle. We read a few. They were called Mrs. Piggle Wiggle and the radish cure, Mrs. Piggle Wiggle and the selfishness cure, Mrs. Piggle wiggle and the tiny bitetaker. They were really good books.

I can't wait till we get to make T-shirts. This was so fun!!! Do you think we'll do that in fourth grade? I hope so.

It was fun wearing P.J.'s to school.

We have a mistery guest and we're trying to find out who is the mistery guest is? We have a few clues. I don't remember what the clues are but I think it might be Mrs. Gayhart. But I'm not quite sure.
I have a mother's day gift for you but I'm not telling what it is.

Love,
Abby

**I am so proud of you and your Academic Fair Project!! WOW, WAY TO GO Abby 1st Place!!! Yeah!!!**

145

## MONTHLY NEWSLETTERS

By third grade, students can begin to write regular columns in the newsletters. Monthly newsletters create a sense of community. They provide parents with an opportunity to preview the curriculum and classroom projects for the upcoming month and recent learning. Monthly newsletters are generally two to three pages in length. They can include features such as: From A Kid's Eye View, Dear Teacher, Monthly Calendar, and Curriculum Overview to inform parents in a fun and interesting manner.

Teachers can involve students in the following way:

1.  During the last 15 - 20 minutes of the day, two or three times a week, students review the day's learning and offer their views about the most important and interesting events.

2.  The teacher lists their responses on the board.

3.  The students then individually choose a topic from the list, and each writes a short descriptive paragraph.

4.  The teacher collects the paragraph and assigns teams to peer edit.

5.  The students peer edit each other's work. They have now become co-authors on two articles.

This activity has several positive features:

❖ It serves as a closure-summarization activity.

❖ Students have an opportunity to practice writing a brief, journalistic text.

❖ Students work together to edit and improve their own and others' writing skills.

❖ Each student in the classroom is co-author of two articles.

❖ Parents receive frequent communication about classroom activities from students' perspective.

Students have a regular and authentic opportunity to publish their work for others to read and appreciate.

**NEWS FLASHES**

There are times when events occur that require immediate publication or an upcoming activity warrants attention, such as reminding parents that students will attend school only a half-day due to parent/teacher conferences or alerting parents that their children will be on the TV news tonight. Teachers may also use news flashes to inform parents about TV programming that is relevant to curriculum the class is currently studying. News Flashes are very brief, but still cover the Who, What, Where, When and Why. For example:

Mr. Arn's fourth grade history students and Ms. Mark's fifth grade students have combined their talents to construct models of the greatest American inventions. The students have also written research papers about the inventors and the origin and historical impact of the invention.

The project reports and models will be displayed in the school Media Center during Science Week (January 10-17). Parents may view the projects on Science Fair Night, Thursday, January 14, from 6:00 - 9:00 p.m.

We hope to see you there.

 Experience has demonstrated that you will need to copy about six extra newsletters and flashes as you will have students of all ages lose them.

Notes:

**Section C**

# PERSONAL INTERACTIONS

Personal interactions are opportunities for parents and teachers to share information about a student's needs in two-way verbal or written conversation.

## PHONE CALLS AND EMAILS

A powerful tool for communicating with parents is the telephone. Unfortunately, phone calls have traditionally been reserved for "bad news." However, successful teachers have found that brief, positive, frequent telephone conversations help to establish a strong partnership with parents (Fredericks & Rasinski, 1990). When parents receive a phone call regarding something exciting happening at school, they immediately sense the teacher's enthusiasm for teaching their son/daughter and are more likely to become involved in classroom activities. Thus, whenever possible, the phone should be used as an instrument of good news. Regardless of the reason the teacher makes the call, it is always important to have the parents' correct surname, as there are many blended families in today's schools. Further, all calls to parents should be documented. The example below is a way to manage and maintain a record of phone conversations.

---

**Sample Phone Call Log**

**Child:** *Robert Romero*     **Parent name:** *Mrs. Rodriquez*     **Phone #:** *555-7272*

**Date:** *Feb. 2*     **Regarding:** *Student has been absent for 3 days*

**Action:** *Robert has chicken pox, he will be out at least 4 more days. Older brother will pick up get well card from class and bring home extra storybooks.*

**Date:** *March 3*     **Regarding:** *Academic progress*

**Action:** *Robert having great success with reading, especially in paired reading. Is hesitant to write during writer's workshop. Teacher will send home writing briefcase and have parents write stories with Robert.*

**Date:** *April 12*     **Regarding:** *Writing progress*

**Action:** *Robert showing more comfort and confidence with his writing. He shared a story he wrote with his parents to the class today.*

---

149

## *Phone Call Log*

| Student | Parent Name | Phone # |
| --- | --- | --- |

Date                    Regarding

Action

Date                    Regarding

Action

Date                    Regarding

Action

*If you are using email, be sure to save all parental communications by creating individual student folders in your electronic mailboxes.

## PROBLEM-SOLVING INTERACTIONS

At the elementary level, the progress review conference is generally scheduled after the first and the third grading periods. However, this is not the only time teachers may need to meet with parents. The following case study illustrates how teacher and parents worked together to help identify and resolve a specific problem in the home that was creating tension in the child's school life.

*Maria* - *Six-and-a-half-year-old Maria Kelly had started her first grade at Broadway School as a very happy young lady. She knew all of the alphabet sounds and symbols and was using invented spelling to write letters to her teacher. Maria attended kindergarten at Broadway School the year before so she had a number of friends both at school and home. Maria smiled easily and enjoyed doing her schoolwork until the middle of October. At this time Maria began to cry easily, had difficulty selecting a book and reading during DEAR (Drop Everything And Read), and couldn't write during writing workshop time. Several days after Maria's behavior suddenly changed, her teacher, Ms. J., called her parents.*

*Mr. and Mrs. Kelly, Maria's parents, came to school the following day. Ms. J. described the change in Maria's behavior and asked the parents if they had any ideas about what may have caused the change in Maria. They revealed that since the first week of October, Maria's grandmother, who had become widowed that summer, moved into the Kelly's house. Since the grandmother was still grieving, both Mr. and Mrs. Kelly were spending a great deal of time in the evening consoling her. Ms. J. asked if Maria's evening or bedtime routines had been altered since her grandma had moved into the house. After thinking for a moment, both parents admitted they had been spending most of their time either talking to Grandmother or talking to each other about her psychological health and financial situation. Before Grandmother moved in, they had regularly watched TV with their daughter and had an established bedtime routine of storybook reading. They had both noticed that even though they were sending Maria to bed at the same time, they often found her awake when they went to bed a couple of hours later.*

*At that point in the discussion, it was becoming clear to the Kellys and Ms. J. that at least part of Maria's problem was related to not getting enough sleep. They reasoned that she might be having difficulty falling asleep because her normal bedtime routines had been disrupted. Mrs. Kelly also felt that Maria, an only child, might be somewhat jealous of the attention her grandmother was receiving.*

*Ms. J. asked the Kellys what they thought they could do to help Maria deal with her feelings and to adjust to the new situation in their home. Both Mr. and Mrs. Kelly felt they needed to resume Maria's normal bedtime routine immediately. Mr. Kelly suggested they could begin to seek counseling. The Kellys wanted Ms. J. to keep them informed of Maria's behavior. Ms. J. suggested that she could send home a personal note with Maria each day for the next two weeks. The Kellys were grateful to Ms. J. for bringing Maria's behavior to their attention. Ms. J. was pleased that the Kellys would be attending to Maria's sleep needs and were very willing to begin to resolve the larger problems.*

Research has consistently demonstrated that parent involvement is positively correlated to student achievement. The teacher's role should be to encourage parental participation in many ways.

 Parents respond more consistently when they receive consistent and frequent communiqués from the classroom teacher.

*Successful teachers share the joys of their class community.*

 Begin to draft your weekly letter as you write your weekly lesson plans. This allows you to review your week and prompt your memory.

**CHAPTER CHECKLIST**

Yes    No    Do you know:

☐    ☐    When Open House or Meet the Teacher evenings are scheduled?

☐    ☐    How you plan to encourage parent participation at open house?

☐    ☐    How you will share information about your teaching philosophy and instructional approach?

Yes    No    Have you decided:

☐    ☐    How often you will send written communication to parents?

☐    ☐    How you will document parental interactions?

☐    ☐    How students will share their views of their learning with their parents?

*Trade Secrets*

## Notes:

154

**Chapter 5**

# DOCUMENTING AND SHARING
# STUDENT PROGRESS

**The teacher is responsible for collecting and documenting
academic and behavioral information for all students.**

# COLLECTING AND ORGANIZING STUDENT INFORMATION

## ESTABLISHING A COMPREHENSIVE ASSESSMENT SYSTEM

What is good work?  As a teacher you may find evaluating students' accomplishments among the most thought-provoking decisions you make.  Your greatest challenge will be to create a comprehensive assessment system that:

❖ Allows students multiple ways to reveal their unique abilities and talents.

❖ Involves students in assessing their progress and establishing learning goals.

❖ Presents a total picture of the student's social and intellectual growth.

❖ Is fair and reflective of the local and national norms of student achievement.

❖ Parents and administrators understand and respect.

The purpose of this section is to offer a number of suggestions about how to establish a comprehensive assessment system and begin the process of documenting students' achievement.  A comprehensive assessment system:

❖ Provides teachers with opportunities to determine the effectiveness of their instruction by observing how students interpret and apply new information.

❖ Considers multiple sources of information and a variety of assessment measures when determining a student's abilities in different content areas.

❖ Teaches students how to assess and become involved in their own learning.

❖ Uses both on-demand (formal) and ongoing (informal) assessment measures to evaluate students' progress.

157

## TYPES OF MEASURES AND TESTS

Assessment measures can be divided into two broad categories, On-Demand and Ongoing. Teachers need to use both to collect information about student's progress (Christie, Enz & Vukelich, 1997).

**On-Demand Assessment** – includes standardized or norm-referenced tests. Created by professionals, these types of tests, usually administered once or twice a year, are designed to indicate to teachers, parents and administrators how much a student achieved compared to other students of the same age or grade level throughout the country. These tests focus on group performance rather than on the achievement of an individual student. However, most parents believe this information is critical. Teachers need to be able to explain to parents how these tests are used and how to interpret the scores.

**Ongoing Assessment** – relies on the regular collection of products that demonstrate each student's knowledge and learning. This information immediately informs the teacher about how well students learned today's instruction. In addition, these assessments inform and guide the teacher's day-to-day instructional decisions. This category of assessment includes:

- ❖ Teacher-constructed, criterion-referenced tests.
- ❖ Students' products, such as written stories, spelling tests.
- ❖ Observation - anecdotal notes and vignettes.
- ❖ Checklists - of target skills.
- ❖ Video and audio tapes.
- ❖ Diagnostic or placement tests, such as a running record.

Likewise, content tests, either professional or teacher-made, can be categorized into two broad types, formative and summative. Though these tests may look identical, they serve different purposes.

**Formative Tests** – measure the student's progress during a set of lessons or learning experiences so that the teacher can provide appropriate feedback and help the students correct errors or misunderstanding. These tests are typically not recorded and not used to make final decisions about student achievement.

**Summative Tests** – are used at the end of a learning unit to measure the progress the student has made over time. These tests are graded, recorded and are used to evaluate a student's achievement.

For example, the weekly spelling list may be given to the class to study on Monday. They take a formative test on Wednesday, which informs the teacher and the students what they are to study. On Friday, the class takes the summative spelling test. The results of the Friday spelling test is recorded in the grade book and becomes a part of the spelling grade.

## REPORT CARDS AND GRADE BOOKS

In your years as a student, you probably experienced moments of anxiety when you received your report cards. As a teacher, you are responsible for summarizing a student's achievement and efforts into one 'neat' single grade. Whether the grade is an 'A' or a '1,' compressed alpha or numeric values cannot adequately describe the complete nature of a student's learning experience or academic performance. Regardless of individual viewpoints on grading systems, the reality is that compressed reporting systems will not soon disappear. As a teacher you must consider how you plan to collect and document multiple forms of information about a student's progress.

The first step to collecting and documenting information about a student's progress is determining what data needs to be collected. Veteran teachers suggest the best place to start is the school's grade level report card. It is important to note that at the elementary level there are often three types of progress indicators: Effort, Achievement and Grade Level. In the reading report card section below, teachers assess student progress for all three "grades" for this subject.

### The Reading Section of a Third Grade Report Card

**Progress Indicators**

| EFFORT | ACHIEVEMENT | GRADE LEVEL |
|---|---|---|
| E=Excels | 1=Outstanding | B=Beyond Level |
| S=Satisfactory | 2=Very Good | G=Grade Level |
| N=Needs Improvement | 3=Satisfactory | L=Lower Level |
| | 4=Having Difficulty | |
| | 5=Having Serious Difficulty | |

| READING | 1st Quarter | 2nd Quarter | 3rd Quarter | 4th Quarter |
|---|---|---|---|---|
| **EFFORT:** | | | | |
| **ACHIEVEMENT:** | | | | |
| **GRADE LEVEL WORK:** | | | | |
| Fluency | | | | |
| Oral | | | | |
| Comprehension | | | | |
| Vocabulary | | | | |
| Independent Reading | | | | |

## CASE STUDY

The following case study reviews Ms. R.'s actions as she determined how she would collect information about each student and how she would quantify this information for the report card.

*Ms. R., a third grade teacher, reviewed the reading curriculum guide and third grade report card with the third grade team. After the team had established a long-term curriculum plan for reading, Ms. R. began to collect information about her third grade students. In addition to their reading levels, Ms. R. wanted to know how her students felt about themselves as readers and what each child liked to read. Since the report card required information about grade level, reading fluency and comprehension, and effort, she knew she would need to collect information that reflected these skills.*

*Ms. R. used checklists, observation notes, placement tests and running records to collect relevant reading data for all of her children. Each week she would review and quantify (grade) the students' products and efforts. Initially this was a time-consuming process. To help save time, Ms. R. created a scoring equivalency chart.*

| Excels | E  = 93-100 = | 1 | (Outstanding) |
|---|---|---|---|
| | E  = 90-93  = | 1- | |
| | E- = 87-89  = | 2+ | (Very Good) |
| Satisfactory | S+ = 83-86 = | 2 | |
| | S  = 80-82 = | 2- | |
| | S  = 77-79 = | 3+ | (Satisfactory) |
| | S  = 73-76 = | 3 | |
| | S- = 70-72 = | 3- | |
| Needs Improvement | N  = 67-69 = | 4+ | (Has Difficulty) |
| | N  = 63-66 = | 4 | |
| | N  = 60- 62 = | 4- | |

Ms. R. recorded the grades, either numeric or alpha, in her grade book. She then placed the students' products or observation information in their working folders.

| | Level | Fluency | Comprehension | Effort | Fluency | Comprehension | Effort | Fluency | Comprehension | Effort | Fluency | Comprehension | Effort | Level | Achievement | Effort | Fluency | Comprehension |
|---|---|---|---|---|---|---|---|---|---|---|---|---|---|---|---|---|---|---|
| Tom | B | 1 | 1 | S | 1 | 1 | S | 1 | 1 | N | 1 | 1 | S | B | 1 | S | 1 | 1 |
| Lydia | L | 3 | 1 | E | 3 | 1 | E | 3 | 1 | E | 2+ | 1 | E | G | 2+ | E | 3 | 1 |

Reported Grades

**Grade Level -** Tom is reading beyond the third grade level. Lydia is still reading at a second grade level (or below grade level). Their teacher, Ms. R., determined their reading levels by using two ongoing assessment measures: a Running Record (Clay, 1979) and a Reading Inventory. (See page 158, Types of Measures & Tests.) Both of these measures offer diagnostic and placement information about Tom's and Lydia's reading performance. The following page presents Tom and Lydia's reading grades.

**Reading Achievement -** Ms. R. determined Tom and Lydia's reading achievement grades by combining the grades they received on oral reading fluency and comprehension. *Oral reading fluency* was assessed through the individualized running records Ms. R. took once every other week. (Ms. R. audiotaped each running record for each child. Each student had a tape cassette.) To obtain the *comprehension* grade, Ms. R. once again relied upon the running record. After each reading, Ms. R. asked the students to retell the story. She also asked prompt questions that stimulated inferential responses. Ms. R. used a "Story Retelling Checklist" to guide her assessments. Tom read fluently and was able to comprehend even the most complex plots. Lydia needed support during oral reading (she had difficulty with multi-syllable words), but she too was able to comprehend story lines and enjoyed relating the characters to people she knew.

**Effort Grade -** Tom and Lydia's effort grades were determined by several factors. First, Ms. R. asked the children to read their assigned pages for Reader's Workshop and respond in their journal at least once each week. Second, Ms. R. observed the children's interactions with literature during DEAR (**D**rop **E**verything **A**nd **R**ead). She recorded and dated these observations. Tom showed satisfactory effort. Occasionally he forgot to read and reflect upon the assigned pages for Reader's Workshop. Several times during DEAR he distracted others. Lydia, on the other hand, read all assigned pages for Reader's Workshop. She wrote thoughtful journal reflections that demonstrated she was working hard to understand the story and characters. During DEAR, Lydia was so deeply engrossed in her stories that Ms. R. often needed to remind Lydia it was time to change activities. Though Lydia began the semester with a second grade reading level, she excelled in her efforts to become a good reader. In fact, at the end of the quarter, Lydia was beginning to read grade level texts.

*Trade Secrets*

## Tom's Reading Grades for the First Quarter

### Progress Indicators

| EFFORT | ACHIEVEMENT | GRADE LEVEL |
|---|---|---|
| E=Excels | 1=Outstanding | B=Beyond Level |
| S=Satisfactory | 2=Very Good | G=Grade Level |
| N=Needs Improvement | 3=Satisfactory | L=Lower Level |
| | 4=Having Difficulty | |
| | 5=Having Serious Difficulty | |

| READING | 1st Quarter | 2nd Quarter | 3rd Quarter | 4th Quarter |
|---|---|---|---|---|
| EFFORT: | B | | | |
| ACHIEVEMENT: | 1 | | | |
| GRADE LEVEL WORK: | S | | | |
| Fluency | 1 | | | |
| Oral | 1 | | | |
| Comprehension | 2 | | | |
| Vocabulary | 1 | | | |
| Independent Reading | 3 | | | |

## Lydia's Reading Grades for the First Quarter

### Progress Indicators

| EFFORT | ACHIEVEMENT | GRADE LEVEL |
|---|---|---|
| E=Excels | 1=Outstanding | B=Beyond Level |
| S=Satisfactory | 2=Very Good | G=Grade Level |
| N=Needs Improvement | 3=Satisfactory | L=Lower Level |
| | 4=Having Difficulty | |
| | 5=Having Serious Difficulty | |

| READING | 1st Quarter | 2nd Quarter | 3rd Quarter | 4th Quarter |
|---|---|---|---|---|
| EFFORT: | L | | | |
| ACHIEVEMENT: | 2+ | | | |
| GRADE LEVEL WORK: | E | | | |
| Fluency | 3 | | | |
| Oral | 1 | | | |
| Comprehension | 2 | | | |
| Vocabulary | 2 | | | |
| Independent Reading | 3 | | | |

## OBSERVATIONS AND ANECDOTAL NOTES

Standardized tests and paper–pencil products offer a narrow view of a student's capabilities. This is especially true of minority, low socioeconomic, and special needs students. A unique feature of the portfolio evaluation system is the extensive use of teacher observation and anecdotal notes to help parents and other educators "see" a more complete portrait of the student's abilities and behavior in class. To help facilitate observation and anecdotal note-taking, teachers may:

* ❖ Distribute several sticky pads throughout your classroom.
* ❖ Observe students interacting with others in learning centers or groups.
* ❖ Describe (not interpret) the event as accurately as possible (on the pad).
* ❖ Date each entry and identify the student you're observing.

After Ms. R. practiced this observation technique, she found she was able to write an anecdotal episode about each student in the classroom two to three times a month. At the end of the week, the teacher collected all the written notes, peeled and placed them, in chronological order, in the student's portfolio.

> Example: Lydia - DEAR 9/26
>
> During DEAR time she began to cry. I asked her what was wrong and she told me she had just read the part where Charlotte died.

## SELECTING STUDENT WORK

Ms. R. had a working folder for each of her students. It contained all their tests and the work for which Ms. R. had recorded grades. From the working folder Ms. R. selected the samples that would represent the typical range of the student's work, as well as the student's best work. This work is then organized in a portfolio.

> Many teachers have the students participate in selecting items for their performance portfolio.

## PORTFOLIO EVALUATION SYSTEM

From the first weeks of school, Ms. R. has collected formal and informal documentation of student progress and placed them in the working folder. The products for the portfolio were selected from the working folder. Ms. R. then:

❖ Used a sturdy two-pocket folder with center tabs that helped to organize observational notes in a sequential manner.

❖ Used the special number (see Student's Code) that corresponds alphabetically to the students' last names. Students write their names in one corner of their work and their number in the other. Using numbers in addition to names allows even kindergartners to help collate and file student work.

❖ Labeled the portfolio with the student's name and number.

❖ Filed all the formal evaluations that she has given, such as standardized test results, unit tests, district criterion-referenced tests, basal placement tests, etc.

❖ Filed all informal tests. These could include reading inventories, running records, teacher-made tests, etc.

❖ Collected and filed all the samples she had of work from all content areas.

In addition to test score results and grades, the portfolio allows Ms. R. an opportunity to document each student's development over time.

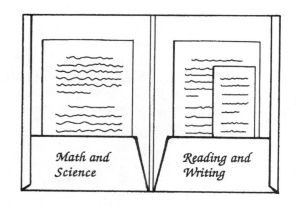 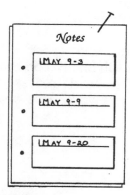

**Teacher files only confidential information;
the student helps file all other materials.**

# PREPARING FOR PARENT-TEACHER CONFERENCES

Successful conferences are the result of careful planning and organization.  A successful conference means that parents and teachers have:

- ❖ Shared information about the student and both have a better understanding and appreciation of the student's needs and abilities.

- ❖ Developed a mutual trust and respect for each other and will continue to work together for the benefit of the student.

## CONFERENCE PLANNING AND SCHEDULING

Begin scheduling conferences *at least two weeks prior* to the first conference dates.  To do this, you will need to make sure that you:

- ❖ Arrange conferences so parents can attend early in the morning, after school or in the evening.

- ❖ Allow 15-20 minutes per conference and schedule at least five minutes between conferences.

- ❖ Establish a first-response, first-scheduled policy.

- ❖ Allow a choice of three time slots in order of preference so that parents may schedule conferences at convenient times. Parents are more likely to attend if they have a choice of time.

- ❖ Include a response confirmation sheet.

When a majority of parents have returned their request, call the parents who have not responded (this saves a great deal of frustration and "paper tag").  After you have scheduled everyone, publish a confirmed schedule listing all appointments, this reminds parents and reaffirms the importance of everyone participating. The following provides an example of a scheduling letter.

 Conferences are physically, intellectually and emotionally demanding.  You may wish to bring nutritious snacks and beverages to sustain your energy.

## *Scheduling Letter*

Dear Parents,

I am looking forward to talking with each of you during Parent/Teacher Conference Week, November 1-5.  Please sign up for the three time slots which are most convenient for you.  To assure you receive the time slot that is best for you, please send in the response form as soon as possible.

Please note that, because of parent-teacher conferences, children will be released at 12:00 p.m. on Thursday and Friday, November 4th and 5th.  If this creates a childcare problem, please call the school office to enroll your child, temporarily, in the after-school program.

Student's Name _____     Teacher _____

Parent's Name _____     Phone # _____

Place a 1, 2 and 3 by your first three choices of conference times.

| Monday AM | Tuesday AM | Wednesday AM | Thursday AM |
|---|---|---|---|
| 7:45 ____ | 7:45 ____ | | 7:45 ____ |
| 8:00 ____ | 8:00 ____ | | 8:00 ____ |
| | | | PM |
| | | | 1:00 ____ |
| | | | 1:15 ____ |
| | | | 1:30 ____ |
| | | | 1:45 ____ |
| | | | 2:30 ____ |
| | | | 2:45 ____ |
| | | | 3:00 ____ |
| | | PM | 3:15 ____ |
| | | 4:00 ____ | 4:00 ____ |
| | | 4:15 ____ | 4:15 ____ |
| | | 4:30 ____ | 4:30 ____ |
| | | 4:45 ____ | 4:45 ____ |
| | | 5:00 ____ | 5:00 ____ |
| | | 6:00 ____ | 6:00 ____ |
| | | 6:15 ____ | 6:15 ____ |
| | | 6:30 ____ | 6:30 ____ |
| | | 6:45 ____ | 6:45 ____ |

## PREPARING FOR PROGRESS REVIEW CONFERENCE

Students of all ages are highly complex, social individuals who must function appropriately in two different worlds, school and home. Parents need to understand how a student uses his social skills to become a productive member in the classroom community. Likewise, teachers need to understand the student's home life and recognize its significant influence on a student's behavior, interests and ability to learn.

Parent/teacher communications reach their full potential when parents and teachers share information about the student from their unique perspectives, value the student's individual strengths and needs, and work together for the benefit of the student. The best opportunity teachers have for engaging parents in this interaction is during the parent/teacher conference. Conferences, which feature a positive two-way exchange, are the result of careful planning and organization. There are generally two types of parent/teacher conferences -- the *pre-established conference* that reviews the student's classroom progress and *spontaneous conferences* that deal with a range of specific concerns that occur throughout the school year.

The Progress Review Conference is an opportunity for both partners to share information about the student's social interactions, emotional maturity, and cognitive development in school and at home. One way to help a parent prepare to be an active member during the conference is a pre-conference questionnaire (Christie, Enz & Vukelich, 1997). The parent questionnaire also gives the teacher a preview of parents' concerns. This allows the teacher time to collect information to be better prepared for the conference. The following page provides an example of a pre-conference questionnaire.

***Students learn to assess their own progress.***

### *Example of Pre-Conference Questionnaire*

Dear Parent,

To help us make the most of our parent/teacher time, I am sending thi
questionnaire to help facilitate our progress review conference. Please read
and complete the questions. If you have any other concerns, list them on th
questionnaire and we will discuss any of your inquiries during our time
together. Please return by: _____.

1.  How would you describe your son/daughter's attitude towards school?

2.  What school activity does your son/daughter most enjoy?

3.  What school activity does your son/daughter least enjoy?

4.  How do you think you can help your son/daughter learn?

5.  Are there any unique situations or problems you want to share to help
    me understand your son/daughter better?

Thank you for your help.

Sincerely,

Teacher's Name

*This may need to be translated into another language.

## SETTING THE SCENE

The day of conferences has arrived. You have scheduled parents and have organized the student portfolios, completed report cards and completed conference format forms. To complete your preparation, consider organizing waiting and conference areas.

**Waiting Area -** On the days of the parent/teacher conferences, you will want to consider providing a waiting area for parents as even the most carefully planned schedule can go awry. Obviously, it is important that your full attention be focused on the parent/s you are currently meeting. Therefore, if possible, the waiting area should be visually and auditorially set apart from the regular classroom.

**Conference Setting -** To encourage positive interaction and promote two-way dialogue, you may consider conducting the conferences at a "neutral" location, such as a table located in a private section of the classroom. Conducting the conference at your desk, with you sitting directly across from the parents, may convey an adversarial message.

 You may need to have a language translator at some conferences; contact district or school office for suggestions.

 In your waiting area, include some of the products the students have created, such as group reports, stories or a classroom photo album.

 Occasionally, a parent might want to know how another student in your class is progressing. It is important for you to remember that this is confidential.

 Staying organized is easier if you keep all student materials in portfolios and all the portfolios in a file box that is close to your conference setting.

**Notes:**

**Section C**

# SHARING STUDENT PROGRESS

During the Progress Review Conference the teacher will, of course, share information about the student's academic progress. Beyond test scores and academic progress, however, most parents also want to know about their son/daughter's social interactions and classroom behavior.

To keep the conference focused and allow time to review all aspects of the student's performance in 15 minutes, it is important to use a structured format during the progress review conference. The structure increases the chance that both the teacher's and parents' concerns are adequately discussed.

*Conferencing with parents helps you learn more about your students.*

171

## PROGRESS REVIEW CONFERENCE PLAN

**Welcome and Positive Statement -** The teacher's first sentence helps establish a foundation for a proactive conference. Positive statements are sincere and usually personal. For example, "Lydia is so eager to learn."

**Three Step Conference Plan -** Next, the teacher should briefly review the three steps of the conference, which include parent input, teacher input and closure.

1.　　*Parent Input* - "First, I am going to ask you to share with me what you have observed about Lydia this year that makes you feel good about her learning and also what concerns you have about her progress."

　　　*(It is important for parents to focus on their son/daughter's academic and social strengths when they meet with you. It is also important for you to know what the parents view as their son/daughter's major academic/social concerns.)*

2.　　*Teacher Input -* "Then, I will share some of Lydia's work with you and my observations about her progress. We'll discuss ideas that will continue to encourage her learning."

　　　*(The success of the parent/teacher relationship depends upon the teacher's ability to highlight the student's academic/social strengths and progress. When area/s of concern are discussed, it is important to provide examples of the student's work or review the observational data to illustrate the point. Often the issues the parents reveal are directly related to the teacher's concerns. Whenever possible, connect these concerns. This reinforces the feeling that the teacher and the parents have the same goals for helping the student grow. It is essential to solicit the parents' views and suggestions for helping the child and also provide concrete examples to help the student improve.)*

3.　　*Closure* - "Finally, we'll summarize the conference by reviewing the home/school activities that will best help Lydia continue to progress."

　　　*(To make sure both teacher and parents have reached a common understanding, it is necessary to briefly review the main ideas and suggestions for improvement that were discussed during the conference.)*

### *Conference Planner*

Student's Name _____ Parent's Name_____

Conference Date _____ Time _____ Other Teachers _____

Welcome and Positive Statement _____

**Review Conference Steps -** Our conference today will consist of three parts. First, I will ask you to review _____ progress, sharing with me both academic/social strengths and areas of concern. Next, I'll review work with you and discuss academic/social strengths and areas in which we will want _____ to grow. Finally, we will discuss the main points we discussed today and review the strategies that will help _____ make progress.

1.  Parent Input - What have you observed about _____ this year that makes you feel good about his/her learning?

    _____

    _____

    _____

    What are your main concerns? _____

    _____

2.  Teacher Input - I would like to share some observations about _____ work and review the areas of strengths and the skills that need to be refined.

    _____

    _____

    _____

3.  Closure - Let's review the things we talked about that will facilitate continued success. _____

    _____

    _____

## STUDENT - PARENT - TEACHER CONFERENCES

A rather new innovation in progress conferences is the inclusion of the student. The students participate equally; sharing their work, discussing areas that he/she has noticed improvement, and establishing academic and/or social goals. This type of conference requires the student to be an active participant in selecting what work will be featured in the portfolio. In addition, the teacher must begin to help students develop the skill to evaluate their own performance.

Since a three-way conference may be a new experience for parents, it is important for the teacher to establish guidelines for parents and students. A letter sent home explaining the format of the conference and discussing each person's role is essential. Parents are encouraged to ask open-ended questions, such as:

> "What did you learn the most about?"
> "What did you work the hardest to learn?"
> "What do you want to learn more about?"

Questions such as these encourage students to analyze their own learning and also help them to set new goals. Parents should not criticize the child's work or focus on any negative aspect of any material that is presented during the conference. Negative comments, particularly from parents, will only inhibit learning and dampen excitement about school.

The following is a brief excerpt of a three-way conference at the last conference of the year. Notice that six-year-old Manuel does most of the talking:

**Mother:** Manuel, what have you worked hardest to learn?

**Manuel:** My writing. I can do it faster and all of my friends can read my stories now. I draw really good ill-stra-suns -- everybody likes them.

**Teacher:** Manuel, can you read your parents a favorite story you wrote?"

**Manuel:** (Manuel begins to read his 5-page, illustrated story with great confidence. He underlines the words with his fingers and reads with great fluency. His parents smile and are impressed with their son's comical pictures.)

**Teacher:** Manuel, what else have you been working on?

**Manuel:** My counting and adding. I can add really good and I helped Shelly and Robbie put together the 100 number board. (Manuel takes his parents over to the 1-100 number board. He is quite proud.)

**Father:** Manuel, what do you want to learn next year?

**Manuel:** I want to read more big books (referring to chapter books). I want to get my own library card. I want to learn the number tables, you know, like Maria (his 4th grade sister) can do. I want to write more books about the Rangers and stuff.

## PROACTIVE STATEMENTS

Sometimes the information you must share about a student is difficult for the parents to hear. How you convey this type of information can "make or break" a conference. Negative statements may cause parents to become defensive and stop listening. Parents will more likely continue to listen if the teacher focuses on the positive and takes a proactive stance. For example, "Joe can pass the class if..." rather than "Joe will fail the class unless...." The following examples provide a negative statement, samples of more positive ways to express the same points and examples of supporting details.

| Teacher's Concern | Negative Statement | Proactive Statement | Supporting Details |
|---|---|---|---|
| Not completing classwork | He wastes half the morning fooling around. | He has so much energy and curiosity that he sometimes has trouble keeping focused on his work. | He talks to his friends and looks to see what others are doing. |
| Insecurity | When something is hard or difficult for him, he won't even try. | He is a good worker when he is familiar with the material. He needs to apply the same habits to unfamiliar material. | When the work is difficult, he asks to leave the room, tears the paper or throws his book on the floor. |
| Poor social skills | If he does not like you, you know it. He makes fun of students who are not in his group. | He is very perceptive; he can identify with other people's strengths as well as their weaknesses. This gives him an edge that he sometimes uses to tease other students. | He knows what makes others uncomfortable and self-conscious (weight, height, braces); he points it out to them (calls them fat, shorty, tinsel teeth). |
| Poor social skills | His peers tease and taunt him, and make him the scapegoat. | He does good work but has trouble gaining the respect of classmates. | The others tease him about his glasses and front teeth. |

## MANAGING FRUSTRATED PARENTS

Unfortunately, even the most prepared and tactful teacher will at one time or another deal with a frustrated or hostile parent. Generally, these parents are upset because they believe their son/daughter is not being treated fairly or given enough attention. The following scenarios illustrate specific types of hostile behavior. The goal in all cases is to diffuse the parent's anger/frustration and begin to develop solutions to improve or resolve the problem. Illustrative examples of what steps you might take to ease the conference to more productive grounds are provided. Teachers can use both verbal and nonverbal communication to respond to the parent's inner feelings by acknowledging the validity of the parent's concerns.

### *Scenario 1*

**Parent:**  "My daughter cries every night. The kids on the playground tease and hurt her. The teacher on duty cannot make the other kids behave. I work and I cannot come to school every day to protect her."

**Teacher:**  "I understand. I would be upset if my daughter cried every night. I will speak to the teacher on playground duty and watch for a few days as well. After I have talked to the duty teacher and observed for a few days, let's talk on the phone again. I'll try to determine why the children are teasing your daughter; then we'll work together on finding a solution."

### *Scenario 2*

**Parent:**  "My son's math has not improved since he was placed with you."

*(Teacher should ignore direct "attack." Instead, focus attention on the student's problem.)*

**Teacher:**  "I'm concerned about his math, too. Let's focus on what we think his academic difficulties are and how we can work together to help him."

Occasionally a parent is so angry and verbally abusive that the present conference cannot accomplish anything constructive. If several attempts to refocus the conference have failed, the teacher needs to calmly end the conference and reschedule another time when the principal may join the discussion.

 It is important for the teacher to recognize that unreasonable hostility may have origins beyond the student's problems at school. Rescheduling the conference allows tempers to cool and time for the teacher to further investigate possible reasons for the parent's aggressive behavior.

**CHAPTER CHECKLIST**

Yes   No

Sharing Student Progress

☐   ☐   Have you developed a conference-scheduling letter?

☐   ☐   Do you have the parents' perspectives of student progress and instructional needs?

☐   ☐   Have you considered the format you will use to conduct the conference?

☐   ☐   Have you considered how (or if) you will incorporate the student in the conference?

☐   ☐   Do you know what types of information you will share with parents?

☐   ☐   Did you develop a management system for storing student work?

*Trade Secrets*

# Notes:

Chapter 6

# TEACHING STUDENTS WITH DIVERSE ABILITIES

**Overview**
- ❖ Teaching Students with Diverse Abilities
- ❖ Case Study: Mark

**Section A:    Common Questions**
- ❖ What Is Special Education?
- ❖ Where Does Special Education Happen?
- ❖ Exceptionalities
- ❖ Referral Processes
- ❖ What Is an Individualized Education Program (IEP)?
- ❖ Information Regarding a Student with an Exceptionality

**Section B:    Special Education Supports**
- ❖ Common Inclusive Collaborative Models
- ❖ Modifications in Curriculum and Instruction
- ❖ Effective Instructional Strategies
- ❖ Common Concerns

**Section C:    Resources:  Who?  Where?  What?**
- ❖ Parents and/or Guardians
- ❖ School or District Personnel
- ❖ Educational Support Teams
- ❖ Glossary

**Chapter Checklist**

**OVERVIEW**

*Teaching Students with Diverse Abilities*

Your students will come in all shapes and sizes. Some will speak English, some will be learning to speak English (Chapter 7), and some may speak through sign language or some other communication device. In the classroom, students will run, walk and roll in wheelchairs. Just as they communicate and move in different ways your students will also learn in different ways.

Special educators in your school will help provide the support for *all* students to be successful in your classroom, the school and the larger community. In order to receive special support for students in your classroom, they must be identified as having an exceptionality. Identification procedures and special education services are governed by specific federal and state legislation.

This chapter addresses some of the questions teachers typically have about teaching students who are receiving special education services. The information in this chapter is illustrated through Mark, an elementary student who has exceptional learning needs. The use of this case study is in no way prescriptive, but merely an example of how the concepts and ideas in this chapter are applicable in a variety of school settings and with different instructional approaches. The goal remains the same -- to create inclusive learning communities in which all children are valued.

*All children can learn with the right support.*

**Case Study: Mark**

*Mark Barger is a seven-year-old student in second grade at Apple Elementary School. Mark is a socially active student who has quite a few friends, likes school and enjoys participation in many extracurricular activities such as scouts and baseball. Because of his gregarious personality, Mark has always been well liked by students, teachers and staff.*

*Mark's mother reported that his medical history was normal at birth. She reported that Mark had severe pneumonia when he was two, but felt there were no negative effects from his illness. In addition, Mrs. Barger reported that Mark seemed very normal as a baby and toddler (e.g., sitting up, crawling, walking) when compared to her other children.*

*Teachers first noticed Mark's learning problems when he was in preschool. Although minor at the time, his inattention and hyperactive behaviors eventually became more prominent as the academic demands increased and his teachers required him to attend to activities for longer periods of time. Despite his academic and behavioral problems, Mark's friendly smile and teacher-pleasing behaviors always seemed to prevent his teachers from giving him poor grades and reporting his minor incidents of misconduct. Often when Mark became too frustrated, he would daydream or sketch.*

*Finally, at the age of seven, Mark's second grade teacher, Mrs. Smith, who had known Mark for some time, initiated a referral. She was surprised that teachers had not referred him earlier. Mrs. Smith referred him for special services because she had observed Mark's inability to read. She also noticed that Mark had a short attention span and was hyperactive. Mark could not remember letters or simple words from one day to the next. He reversed several letters. Although his handwriting was legible when copying, he was unable to write or spell a given letter or simple word recalled a short time later. Mark was diagnosed as having learning disabilities specifically in reading, writing and spelling.*

*Mrs. Barger felt that all of the pieces to the puzzle were beginning to fit into place. She was relieved to learn that Mark qualified to receive special services earlier that year. Although she still did not agree with the label of learning disabled, she was happy to see him finally get some help. He was in a regular second grade classroom. His special education teacher, Mr. Roland, visited him daily in his class to work on reading skills. Mrs. Smith spent extra time with him before and after school, providing him with extra practice opportunities on skills. Peer and cross-aged tutors also provided short lessons with Mark.*

*Besides drawing, Mark demonstrated above-average intelligence in mathematics. He often solved his fifth grade sister's math problems after she read the story problems aloud. Mark's father reported that he could solve complex puzzles and games (checkers, chess, trivia, etc.) quicker than his older brother and sister.*

*Trade Secrets*

## Notes:

182

**Section A**

## COMMON QUESTIONS

### WHAT IS SPECIAL EDUCATION?

The Education for all Handicapped Children Act was passed in 1975, amended in 1986 and 1992, and re-authorized as the Individuals with Disabilities Education Act (IDEA) in 1991 and 1997. It established the right to a free and appropriate public education (FAPE) in the least restrictive environment (LRE) for children with exceptionalities. The law mandates that each student receiving special educational services have an Individual Education Plan (IEP). The IEP is a written document developed by a multidisciplinary team which includes the student, the student's parents (guardian), the student's regular and special education teachers, and other school administrative and support personnel. It describes the student's current level of functioning, their goals and objectives, the types of support the student needs and the dates for the initiation and duration of that support. Students may need intermittent or sustained support services. These supports may be limited to particular environments or pervade all aspects of the student's life. Examples of the educational supports provided for Mark will be described in Section B of this chapter.

*Learning how to support all students is your responsibility and challenge.*

**Continuum of Educational Services for Students with Exceptionalities from Least to Most Restrictive**

General education classroom with
consultation from specialists

General education classroom with
collaboration from specialists

Part-time placement in special education class

Full-time special education class in general
education school

Special education school

Residential school,
treatment center,
homebound

**WHERE DOES SPECIAL EDUCATION HAPPEN?**

Educational placements for students with special needs range from the most restrictive, hospitalization, to the least restrictive, the regular classroom. Special education supports are sometimes delivered in a specific place, either removed from the regular classroom or within the classroom. However, special education is not a place; rather, it is the range of supports designed to meet the needs of students challenged with special learning needs. Since 1975 several trends have been witnessed in special education:

* Classrooms and schools have become more inclusive and less segregated.

  o *Example: Children with physical exceptionalities are included in general education.*

* Curriculum has focused more on higher-level outcomes and problem solving in naturally occurring situations and less on remediation.

  o *Example: Children with exceptionalities are included instructionally in general education.*

* Classrooms have evolved into caring communities of diverse learners.

  o *Example: Children with exceptionalities are included socially in general education.*

* Regular education teachers, special education teachers, parents, and school staff work together as problem-solving teams.

  o *Example: Collaboration is a critical component empowering educators to maintain inclusive educational environments for all students.*

The trend toward including all students in regular classrooms with the special education supports they need to be successful has been called the inclusion movement. Regular education classrooms in which general and special educators work together to meet all students' physical, instructional and social needs at least 80% of their school day are considered inclusive classrooms (U.S. Department of Education, 1994).

*Mark spends his day in a regular second grade classroom. His teacher collaborates and co-teaches with the special education teacher during language arts.*

185

## EXCEPTIONALITIES

### *Types of Exceptionalities*

There are 12 categories of exceptionality identified by the federal government. These categories and their names may vary somewhat from state to state:

- ❖ Mental retardation
- ❖ Specific learning disabilities
- ❖ Serious emotional disturbances
- ❖ Speech or language impairments
- ❖ Hearing impairments
- ❖ Visual impairments

- ❖ Deaf blindness
- ❖ Orthopedic impairments
- ❖ Other health problems
- ❖ Multiple disabilities
- ❖ Autism
- ❖ Traumatic brain injury

States also offer special educational supports for students identified as gifted and talented, and students having academic difficulty who may be labeled "at risk." You must remember, however, that categorical labels have limited instructional value, serving primarily as a means for allocating federal funds to pay for special education services. The U.S. Department of Education (1995) developed definitions for each of these categories (pages 213-216) and each state has developed different rules and regulations specifying implementation procedures to comply with the Individuals with Disabilities Education Act.

*Mark was identified as having specific learning disabilities in reading, writing and spelling.*

### *Causes of Exceptionalities*

Usually there are several interrelated variables which may result in an individual having an exceptionality. Contributing factors may include heredity, environment or a combination of the two. General causes of some exceptionalities are:

- ❖ Genetic (e.g., Down Syndrome).
- ❖ Metabolic (e.g., phenylketonuria or PKU).
- ❖ Environmental factors (e.g., lead poisoning, fetal alcohol syndrome).
- ❖ Chronic illness (e.g., asthma, diabetes, HIV).
- ❖ Brain injury (e.g., asphyxia).
- ❖ Accidents (e.g., spinal cord injuries).
- ❖ Congenital birth defects (e.g., spina bifida, cerebral palsy).

The important task for the teacher is to focus on providing the necessary support for students to be successful in the classroom, rather than trying to determine the exact cause of an exceptionality.

## REFERRAL PROCESSES

### *What Do You Do If You Think a Student Needs Special Education Services?*

Before you make a formal referral to someone in your special education department about a student who may be a candidate for special services, check your district and state guidelines. According to most guidelines, you are required to do the following:

1. Experiment using a few *procedural or instructional modifications.* (See Section B of this chapter.)

2. Consult with other professionals. Many elementary schools have *pre-referral assistance teams (PAT),* which commonly comprise four or five professionals: other classroom teachers, a special or remedial educator, a counselor, a principal or vice-principal and perhaps a communication disorders specialist. One or more of the PAT members might observe your student in your classroom and collaborate with you to develop alternative strategies (Vaughn, Bos & Schumm, 1997).

3. Initiate a *formal referral* through special education.

*For instance, Mark's teacher went through the pre-referral process which resulted in an initial formal referral.*

187

### What Is a Formal Referral and Identification Process for Special Education?

A referral for a special education evaluation can be initiated by a classroom teacher, by other school personnel or by a parent. Assessments are conducted by a special education *multidisciplinary team (MDT)*. For example, Mark's MDT team included a regular second grade teacher, a special education teacher and a school psychologist. This team may also include a communication disorders specialist, a counselor, a behavioral interventionist, among other professionals. Approved instruments and procedures are used to evaluate the referred student's current levels of functioning in the following areas:

- ❖ *Instructional* (general intelligence, academic performance, communication).

- ❖ *Physical* (motor abilities, health, vision and hearing).

- ❖ *Social* (social-emotional functioning).

After the assessment results are collected, the team shares the results of the assessments with the parent/s. In collaboration with the parent(s) and the classroom teacher, the team determines whether the student in question qualifies for special education services according to federal and state guidelines. To be eligible to receive special education services, a student must meet the eligibility criteria for at least one of the categories (e.g., specific learning disabilities, as in the case of Mark).

## WHAT IS AN INDIVIDUALIZED EDUCATION PROGRAM (IEP)?

Individualized Education Programs are mandated by law for each student who is receiving special education services. The IEP provides a written document that describes the following sections:

1. Present educational level.

2. Planned goals and objectives.

3. Type and location of support services.

4. The extent to which the student will be in regular classroom or other natural environments with students without exceptionalities.

5. Date for initiation and duration of special education services.

6. Procedures to evaluate student's progress.

7. Description of Least Restrictive Environment.

8. Transition services.

*See the following snapshot of Mark's IEP.*

**Mark's IEP Snapshot**

| Date of IEP Meeting:<br>*10-5* | Anticipated Duration of IEP:<br>*October*  to  *October* | IEP Type:<br>☐ Initial  ☒ Annual  ☐ Interim |
| --- | --- | --- |

| | |
| --- | --- |
| Student: *Mark Barger*<br>School: *Apple Elementary*<br>Grade: *2*<br>Current Placement: *Regular Class/Sp Ed Consultant/Co- teacher*<br>Birthdate: *July 17*<br>Address: | District Representative: *Dr. Ryan, Principal*<br>Regular Education Teacher: *Mrs. Smith, 2nd Grade*<br>Special Education Teacher: *Mr. Roland*<br>Parent(s): *Rene & Bob Barger*<br>Evaluator: *Dr. Duffy, Psychologist*<br>Student: *Mark Barger*<br>Other/s: |

| Present Educational Level | Annual Goal | Instructional Objectives | Evaluation |
| --- | --- | --- | --- |
| Language Arts:<br>Strengths<br>1. Can successfully retell short stories in sequence, often elaborating, creating additional details.<br>2. Writes legibly when copying manuscript.<br>3. Talented artist.<br><br>Weaknesses<br>1. Frequently unable to recall names or sounds of letters, letter combinations and words.<br>2. Reverses and inverts letters.<br>3. Unable to spell one-syllable words.<br>4. Does not complete assignments. | Mark will demonstrate improvement in Language Arts Skills by 4-6 months. | 1. When presented with letters (consonants/short and long vowel combinations), Mark will say name and sounds correctly, 40-60/minute.<br>2. When dictated sounds (consonants/short and long vowel combinations), words or phonetically controlled sentences, Mark will write (spell) the letter/s, words or sentences correctly 40-60 letters/minute and 15 words/minute.<br>3. When presented with phonetic-controlled words, Mark will sound blend words at a rate of 80-100 words/minute with 90% accuracy.<br>4. When presented with phonetic-controlled stories, Mark will read 200 words/minute.<br>5. Mark will dictate original stories incorporating words with lesson's sounds with a minimum of 5 sentences. | Daily charting. Teacher and Mark self-monitor<br><br>↓<br><br>Journal and Portfolio |

### *What Roles Do Teachers, Students, and Parents Play in the Development and Implementation of IEPs?*

Both the general education teacher and the special education teacher should actively participate in writing and implementing the student's plan. Parents must be invited to the IEP meeting. The team should attempt to accommodate the parents' schedule when holding these meetings. It is vital that the parents participate in designing every component of the document. They should understand the process, including the transition plans between elementary and high school, high school and college, and high school and work. Parents should also work with support staff and help develop transportation plans. Parents should understand their right to contest or appeal any feature of their child's IEP. When appropriate, the student should also be actively involved in preparing the team plan.

*Mark participated in his IEP development.*

## INFORMATION REGARDING A STUDENT WITH AN EXCEPTIONALITY

Ideally, you will have been an active participant in the multidisciplinary team IEP meeting when the supports necessary for your student were developed. Time and personnel constraints may have precluded your participation, in which case, consult with your special education staff to obtain:

- ❖ A "snapshot" of the student's IEP containing the goals and objectives.

- ❖ The level of support you will be given to help meet the needs of a student with exceptionalities placed in your classroom.

- ❖ Your student's interests and any items or events in which they enjoy participating.

- ❖ Academic performance and instructional approaches from which the student has benefited.

- ❖ Behavioral approaches that have been successful in promoting responsible self-determination.

- ❖ Medications your student may be taking and medical problems that could interfere with his/her education (e.g., seizures, asthma attacks).

**Section B**

# SPECIAL EDUCATION SUPPORTS

***Where do I go?***

Traditionally, special education and regular education have been separate programs housed in separate places. A continuum of placements for students with exceptionalities has ranged from hospitalization or homebound, to separate schools, separate classes, pull-out classes and the regular class. Regular education teachers typically had students with exceptionalities pulled from their classes at predetermined times for specific instruction in special education classrooms.

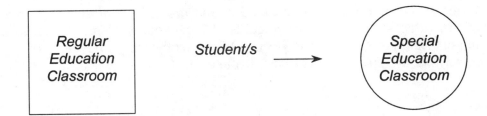

The trend toward providing special education supports within regular, heterogeneous classrooms, has spawned a variety of delivery models. There are no specific roadmaps for schools to follow as they develop inclusive, heterogeneous classes. Each community of professionals, students and parents works to develop the route that works best for them. The ways you include students physically, instructionally and socially will depend on the type of support model used in your school and the collaborative relationships you establish with the school's special education and resource professionals.

## COMMON INCLUSIVE COLLABORATIVE MODELS

There are six models commonly used in schools (Montgomery, 1996). All are flexible and continually adapt to the needs of changing students, faculty and staff.

### *Collaborative Support*

Students with exceptionalities are included in regular, heterogeneous classrooms. Each class may have two to three students with exceptionalities. This corresponds to the natural proportion of occurrence of individuals with those exceptionalities in the general population. Special educators, instructional assistants and other support professionals come into the classroom as necessary to support students. These professionals are "pulled into" the regular classroom, rather than routinely "pulling out" students for instruction. This does not preclude students leaving the class from time to time for work that requires conditions not possible in the regular classroom.

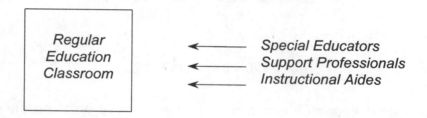

### *Blended Classrooms*

A regular education classroom and a special education classroom serving students of similar ages combine their classes. This allows the regular classroom teacher to provide expert curricular-content knowledge and the special educator to make specific instructional adaptations to ensure students with exceptionalities can access the regular curriculum. Blended classes can occur at both elementary and secondary levels and may or may not require larger classroom space.

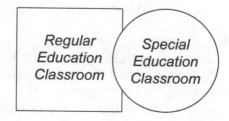

### *Clustered Aides*

In this model, instructional aides support students in regular classes according to a schedule that meets the instructional and grouping demands of those classes. Collaboration among the regular educators allows for flexible grouping and re-grouping of students to maximize utilization of the instructional aides. This provides opportunities for individual and small group instruction, as well as monitoring large groups during various daily activities. This array of aides is associated with the students with exceptionalities and moves through the school system with them. It is not tied to any specific grade level in the school.

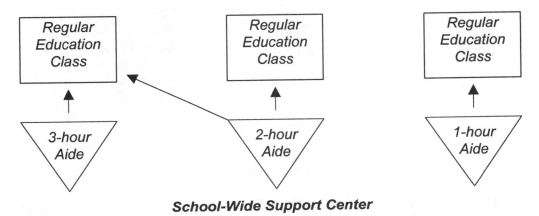

### *School-Wide Support Center*

The establishment of a school-wide support center centralizes all members of the special education team in one large area. They all have their desks, files and instructional areas in the center. Students served by the special education team may come into the center for individualized instruction and the team members go out into the regular classrooms to collaboratively team- and co-teach with regular educators. It requires both trust and collaboration among the professionals involved, merging the expertise of all educators to meet the needs of all students.

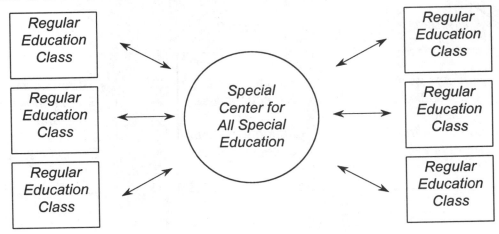

193

### Three-Part Schedules

This model is more typical for upper grades. Students with exceptionalities choose classes from the core subjects and electives available to all students, supplementing their program with support center classes.

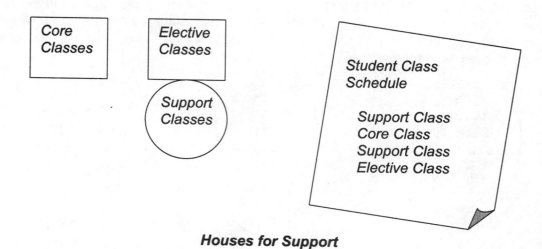

### Houses for Support

Comprehensive middle schools can be organized into "houses" that serve students with and without exceptionalities. General and special education teachers share responsibilities for teaching integrated, interdisciplinary courses. Special educators stay with their students throughout their school career, facilitating the development and maintenance of natural support systems through clubs and other school activities.

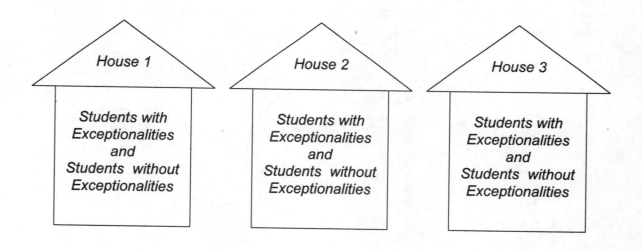

### *What Is the Model at Your School?*

Find out the model used in your school and work with the special education faculty and staff to help support the students in your classroom. Because each school is different and you and your special education faculty are unique, there is no generic way to develop a model of services and teaching configurations within that model.

If you choose to collaborate with your support staff, it is important to establish the shared and individual responsibilities you will assume for your students. Setting aside planning time to decide who will modify the curriculum and management plans, who will be involved in content presentation and who will assign grades will make everyone more comfortable with their role. It is important to remember that different people have different comfort levels as they teach and manage classrooms. You and your collaborative partner/s will need to negotiate your roles so that your partnership capitalizes on each of your unique strengths. Your planning approach must be flexible and allow you to find the fit that compliments your particular blend of styles, personalities and educational philosophies.

*An example of a collaborative/consultative planning grid (Hines & Johnston, 1996) was developed for the student in our case study. Mark's special education teacher and regular education teacher decided to collaboratively co-teach in the regular education classroom during the language arts period. Both teachers were comfortable using a diagnostic-prescriptive approach to curriculum adaptation. A weekly planning period of 45 minutes was set aside and evaluation tools consisted of daily behavior charts, student portfolios and journals.*

### *Collaborative/Consultative Planning Grid*

| Student: Mark Barger | | Grade: 2 | Subject: Language Arts | |
|---|---|---|---|---|
| **What?** | **Who?** | **When?** | **Where?** | **How?** |
| **Planning** | Mrs. Smith Mr. Roland SPE | Weekly Thursday 2:15-3:00 | Second Grade Class | Conference Write lessons plan |
| **Curriculum** General/Special Ed. | Both | Daily before school | | Conference |
| **Behavior Management** General/Special Ed. | Both plus Mark | 2X/Weekly | | Conference Charity/Contract |
| **Content Presentation** General/Special Ed. | Both | Daily week | | Direct Instruction Cooperative Groups Learning Contracts and Comps |
| **Evaluation** General/Special Ed. | Both plus Mark | Daily | | Daily Charity Daily Progress Notes Portfolio Journal |

## Collaborative/Consultative Planning Grid

| Student: | | Grade: | Subject: | |
|---|---|---|---|---|
| **What?** | **Who?** | **When?** | **Where?** | **How?** |
| **Planning** | | | | |
| **Curriculum**<br>General/Special Ed. | | | | |
| **Behavior Management**<br>General/Special Ed. | | | | |
| **Content Presentation**<br>General/Special Ed. | | | | |
| **Evaluation**<br>General/Special Ed. | | | | |

| Student: | | Grade: | Subject: | |
|---|---|---|---|---|
| **What?** | **Who?** | **When?** | **Where?** | **How?** |
| **Planning** | | | | |
| **Curriculum**<br>General/Special Ed. | | | | |
| **Behavior Management**<br>General/Special Ed. | | | | |
| **Content Presentation**<br>General/Special Ed. | | | | |
| **Evaluation**<br>General/Special Ed. | | | | |

**MODIFICATIONS IN CURRICULUM AND INSTRUCTION**

Modifying the curriculum content or the instructional strategies in any general education classroom can be accomplished through creative thinking and diligent collaboration between the general educator and the special educators. Effective collaboration can facilitate the purpose of modification: to enable an individual student to compensate for instructional, physical or social challenges. Modifications allow the student to use existing skill repertoires while promoting the acquisition of new skills and knowledge. Instruction is often modified to allow for partial participation. This implies some level of active involvement in a lesson activity acknowledging that not all students learn the same material in the same way (Bradley, Sears & Tessier-Switlick, 1997).

As you view the curriculum and the diversity of the student needs in the classroom, you may sometimes feel overwhelmed about what can be changed. The table below describes four areas in which modifications can be made.

### *Types of Instructional Modifications*

**Adapt Instructional Strategies**

Vary presentation techniques, pacing, assignments and tests adaptations.

**Use Materials and Devices**

Use portable devices or materials that enhance an individual's performance. Items may be commercial or teacher made. Adaptive devices and communication tools, as well as alternative text materials, fall in this category.

**Use of Social Supports**

Use any self-management tools to organize instructional activities. Use any type of verbal, physical, supervisory support, peer buddies, tutors or personal assistants. This assistance may be necessary for long or short time frames.

**Adapt the Environment**

Change the actual physical environment; move furniture and obtain smaller chairs, ramps or use wheelchair-accessible facilities.

Source: Adapted from Ottlinger, K., & Kohlhepp, P. (1992). Curricular Adaptations: Accommodating the Instructional Needs of Diverse Learners in the Context of General Education. Kansas State Board of Education.

*Checklists of possible modifications (Dyck, Pemberton, Woods & Sundbye, 1997; Curriculum Solutions, 1996) have been completed for Mark.*

## *Sample Curriculum Modification Checklist*
*Check ☒ all modifications that are appropriate and necessary for this student.*

STUDENT <u>Mark Barger</u>  DOB <u>7/17</u>  Date <u>10/05</u>  Completed by <u>Ms. Smith and Mr. Roland</u>

### INSTRUCTIONAL STRATEGIES

**Presentation of Subject Matter**
- ☐ Teach to student's learning style
  - ☐ Linguistic  ☐ Logical/Math  ☐ Musical
  - ☐ Spatial  ☐ Bodily/Kinesthetic  ☐ Interpersonal
  - ☐ Experiential Learning  ☐ Multi-sensory
- ☒ Utilize specialized curriculum_____
- ☐ Teacher tape lectures/discussions for replay
- ☐ Provide notes: teacher or peer copy
- ☐ Functional application of academic skills
- ☐ Present demonstrations (model)
- ☐ Utilize manipulatives
- ☐ Emphasize critical information
- ☐ Pre-teach vocabulary
- ☒ Make/use vocabulary files
- ☒ Reduce language level of reading level of assignment
- ☐ Use total communication
- ☐ Use facilitated communication
- ☐ Share activities
- ☐ Use visual sequences
- Other_____

**Pacing**
- ☐ Adjust time requirements
- ☐ Vary activity often
- ☒ Allow breaks
- ☐ Omit assignments requiring copy in timed situation
- ☐ School texts sent home for summer preview
- ☐ Home set of texts/materials for preview/review
- Other_____

**Assignments**
- ☐ Give directions in small, distinct steps:
  - ☐ Rewrite  ☐ Use picture  ☐ Verbalize
- ☐ Use written back-up for oral directions
- ☐ Lower difficulty level
- ☐ Shorten assignment
- ☒ Reduce paper and pencil tasks
- ☒ Read or tape record directions
- ☒ Use pictorial directions
- ☐ Give extra cues or prompts
- ☒ Allow student to record or type assignment
- ☒ Adapt worksheets, packets
- ☐ Utilize compensatory procedures by providing alternate assignment strategy when demands of class conflict with student capabilities
- ☐ Avoid penalizing for spelling errors
- ☐ Avoid penalizing for penmanship or sloppiness
- Other_____

**Testing Adaptations**
- ☒ Oral  ☒ Taped
- ☒ Use visuals
- ☐ Preview language of test questions
- ☐ Applications in real setting
- ☐ Test administered by resource person
- ☐ Modify format: ☐ short ans ☐ mult choice
  - ☐ essay ☐ discussion ☐ T/F
- ☐ adjust time ☐ adjust length
- Other_____

### SOCIAL SUPPORTS

**Self-management/Follow-through**
- ☒ Visual daily schedule
- ☐ Calendars
- ☐ Check often for comprehension/review
- ☐ Request parent reinforcement
- ☐ Have student repeat directions
- ☐ Teach study skills
- ☐ Use study sheets to organize material
- ☐ Design/write/use long term assignment timelines
- ☐ Review and practice in real situations
- ☐ Plan for generalizations
- ☐ Teach skill in several settings/environments
- Other_____

**Social Interaction Support**
- ☒ Personal advocacy
- ☒ Peer tutoring
- ☐ Structure activities to promote social interaction
- ☐ Focus social process instead of activity/end product
- ☐ Structure shared experiences in school/extracurricular
- ☒ Cooperative learning groups
- ☒ Multiple/rotating peers
- ☐ Teach friendship skills/sharing/negotiation
- ☐ Teach social communication skills
- Other_____

**Motivation and Reinforcement**
- ☐ Verbal
- ☐ Non-verbal
- ☐ Positive reinforcement
- ☐ Concrete reinforcement_____
- ☐ Plan motivating sequences of activities
- ☐ Reinforce initiation
- ☐ Offer choice
- ☐ Emphasize strengths/interests
- Other <u>Charting self growth</u>

### ENVIRONMENT
- ☐ Preferential seating
- ☐ Plan Seating ☐ Bus ☐ Classrm ☐ Lunch ☐ Auditorium
- ☐ Alter physical room arrangement
- ☐ Define areas concretely
- ☐ Reduce distractions__Visual__Auditory__Spatial__Motion
- ☐ Teach positive rules for use of space
- ☐ Contracts
- Other <u>Charting - Self – Growth</u>

### MATERIAL AND DEVICES
- ☐ Arrangement of material on page
- ☒ Taped texts and/or other materials: science and math
- ☐ Highlighted texts/study guides
- ☐ Use supplementary materials
- ☐ Note-taking assistance
- ☐ Type teacher material
- ☐ Large print
- ☐ Special Equipment: ☐ electric typewriter ☐ computer
  - ☐ calculator ☐ phone adaptations ☐ video recorder
- ☐ Community Resources
- Other <u>Tape recorder, audio card reader</u>

## Curriculum Modification Checklist

*Check ☒ all modifications that are appropriate and necessary for this student.*

STUDENT_____ DOB _____ DATE _____ COMPLETED BY _____

### INSTRUCTIONAL STRATEGIES

**Presentation of Subject Matter**
- ☐ Teach to student's learning style
  - ☐ Linguistic  ☐ Logical/Math  ☐ Musical
  - ☐ Spatial  ☐ Bodily/Kinesthetic  ☐ Interpersonal
  - ☐ Experiential Learning  ☐ Multi-sensory
- ☐ Utilize specialized curriculum_____
- ☐ Teacher tape lectures/discussions for replay
- ☐ Provide notes: teacher or peer copy
- ☐ Functional application of academic skills
- ☐ Present demonstrations (model)
- ☐ Utilize manipulatives
- ☐ Emphasize critical information
- ☐ Pre-teach vocabulary
- ☐ Make/use vocabulary files
- ☐ Reduce language level of reading level of assignment
- ☐ Use total communication
- ☐ Use facilitated communication
- ☐ Share activities
- ☐ Use visual sequences
- Other_____

**Pacing**
- ☐ Adjust time requirements
- ☐ Vary activity often
- ☐ Allow breaks
- ☐ Omit assignments requiring copy in timed situation
- ☐ School texts sent home for summer preview
- ☐ Home set of texts/materials for preview/review
- Other_____

**Assignments**
- ☐ Give directions in small, distinct steps:
  - ☐ Rewrite  ☐ Use picture  ☐ Verbalize
- ☐ Use written back-up for oral directions
- ☐ Lower difficulty level
- ☐ Shorten assignment
- ☐ Reduce paper and pencil tasks
- ☐ Read or tape record directions
- ☐ Use pictorial directions
- ☐ Give extra cues or prompts
- ☐ Allow student to record or type assignment
- ☐ Adapt worksheets, packets
- ☐ Utilize compensatory procedures by providing
  alternate assignment strategy when demands of class
  conflict with student capabilities
- ☐ Avoid penalizing for spelling errors
- ☐ Avoid penalizing for penmanship or sloppiness
- Other_____

**Testing Adaptations**
- ☐ Oral  ☐ Taped
- ☐ Use visuals
- ☐ Preview language of test questions
- ☐ Applications in real setting
- ☐ Test administered by resource person
- ☐ Modify format: ☐ short ans  ☐ mult choice
- ☐ essay  ☐ discussion  ☐ T/F
- ☐ adjust time  ☐ adjust length
- Other_____

### SOCIAL SUPPORTS

**Self-management/Follow-through**
- ☐ Visual daily schedule
- ☐ Calendars
- ☐ Check often for comprehension/review
- ☐ Request parent reinforcement
- ☐ Have student repeat directions
- ☐ Teach study skills/use study sheets to organize
- ☐ Design/write/use long term assignment timelines
- ☐ Review and practice in real situations
- ☐ Plan for generalizations
- ☐ Teach skill in several settings/environments
- Other_____

**Social Interaction Support**
- ☐ Personal advocacy
- ☐ Peer tutoring
- ☐ Structure activities to promote social interaction
- ☐ Focus social process instead of activity/end product
- ☐ Structure shared experiences in school/extracurricular
- ☐ Cooperative learning groups
- ☐ Multiple/rotating peers
- ☐ Teach friendship skills/sharing/negotiation
- ☐ Teach social communication skills
- Other_____

**Motivation and Reinforcement**
- ☐ Verbal
- ☐ Non-verbal
- ☐ Positive reinforcement
- ☐ Concrete reinforcement_____
- ☐ Plan motivating sequences of activities
- ☐ Reinforce initiation
- ☐ Offer choice
- ☐ Emphasize strengths/interests
- Other_____

### ENVIRONMENT
- ☐ Preferential seating
- ☐ Plan Seating ☐ Bus ☐ Classrm ☐ Lunch/Auditorium
- ☐ Alter physical room arrangement
- ☐ Define areas concretely
- ☐ Reduce distractions_Visual_Auditory_Spatial_Motion
- ☐ Teach positive rules for use of space
- ☐ Contracts
- Other_____

### MATERIAL AND DEVICES
- ☐ Arrangement of material on page
- ☐ Taped texts and/or other materials
- ☐ Highlighted texts/study guides
- ☐ Use supplementary materials
- ☐ Note-taking assistance
- ☐ Type teacher material
- ☐ Large print
- ☐ Special Equipment: ☐ electric typewriter ☐ computer
  ☐ calculator ☐ phone adaptations ☐ video recorder
- ☐ Community Resources
- Other_____

## *Incorporating Modifications Into Daily Schedules*

To begin to plan effectively to incorporate curriculum and instructional modifications for students with exceptionalities into your classroom, it is helpful to compile an overview of the goals in the student's IEP "snapshot" in relationship to the breadth of your regular curriculum and general supports you have developed from the modification checklist. A daily scheduling matrix (Giangreco, Cloninger & Iverson, 1993) is a simple way to incorporate IEP goals from the IEP snapshot into the breadth of the regular curriculum covered in the activities of your class. The general supports and modifications needed by your student can be listed with check marks indicating when they are necessary during regular class activities.

*A sample daily scheduling matrix was developed for Mark. Mark's specific IEP goals were listed and the daily class activities in which they will be addressed were indicated with check marks.*

❖ *The majority of Mark's IEP goals were met during the second grade language arts class.*

❖ *The special educator co-taught and facilitated cooperative learning groups, peer tutoring, learning centers and independent activities to assist Mark in achieving his specific goals and objectives.*

❖ *During other areas of the curriculum, Mark required both technical and physical supports to also ensure success. Technical supports included a tape recorder, an audio card reader and voice-activated computer programs.*

*IEP Meeting*

## Sample Daily Scheduling Matrix

| | Subject | Arrive | Cur. Event | Lang. Arts | Math | Lunch | Recess | Science | S.S. | Art | Music | P.E. | Homework |
|---|---|---|---|---|---|---|---|---|---|---|---|---|---|
| | Time | 7:45 | 8:30 | 9:00 | 10:45 | 11:30 | 12:00 | 1:00 | 1:30 | F 2:00 | TTh 2:00 | MW 2:00 | |
| IEP Goals | Read | | | ✓ | | | | | | | | | |
| | Spell | | | ✓ | | | | | | | | | |
| | Write Sentences | | | ✓ | | | | | | | | | |
| | Write Paragraphs | | | ✓ | | | | | | | | | |
| | Complete Assignment | | | ✓ | ✓ | | | ✓ | ✓ | ✓ | | ✓ | ✓ |
| | Work Coop. in Groups | ✓ | ✓ | ✓ | ✓ | | ✓ | ✓ | ✓ | ✓ | | ✓ | |
| | Work Independently | | | ✓ | ✓ | | | | | ✓ | | ✓ | |
| | Completes Assignment | | | ✓ | ✓ | | | ✓ | ✓ | ✓ | | ✓ | ✓ |
| Breadth of Curriculum | Academics | | | ✓ | ✓ | | | ✓ | ✓ | ✓ | | ✓ | |
| | Physical Education | | | | | | ✓ | | | | | ✓ | |
| | Computer | | ✓ | ✓ | ✓ | | | | | | | | |
| | Communication | → → → → → → → → → → → → → → → → → → → → → → → → → → → → → → → → → → → → → → → → → → → → → | | | | | | | | | | | |
| | Socialization | | | | | | ✓ | | | | | | |
| General Supports | Personal Needs | | | | | | | | | | | | Contract |
| | Materials | | | tape recorder | computer | | | tape recorder | | | | | |
| | Physical Needs | | | | computer desk | | | | | | | | |
| | Teaching Others | | | peer buddy | | | | peer buddy | | | | | |

Student: Mark Barger   Grade: 2

Adapted from Giangreco, M.F. (1993). *Choosing Options and Accommodations for Children*. Baltimore: Brookes Publishing Co.

## Daily Scheduling Matrix

| Student: | | | | | Grade: | | | | | | | |
|---|---|---|---|---|---|---|---|---|---|---|---|---|
| Subject | | | | | | | | | | | | |
| Time | | | | | | | | | | | | |

| | | | | | | | | | | | | |
|---|---|---|---|---|---|---|---|---|---|---|---|---|
| **IEP Goals** | | | | | | | | | | | | |
| | | | | | | | | | | | | |
| | | | | | | | | | | | | |
| | | | | | | | | | | | | |
| | | | | | | | | | | | | |
| | | | | | | | | | | | | |
| | | | | | | | | | | | | |
| **Breadth of Curriculum** | | | | | | | | | | | | |
| | | | | | | | | | | | | |
| | | | | | | | | | | | | |
| | | | | | | | | | | | | |
| **General Supports** | | | | | | | | | | | | |
| | | | | | | | | | | | | |
| | | | | | | | | | | | | |
| | | | | | | | | | | | | |

Adapted from Giangreco, M.F. (1993). *Choosing Options and Accommodations for Children*. Baltimore: Brookes Publishing Co.

### *Incorporating Modifications into Regular Lesson Plans*

Your regular lesson plans and instructional units can be given added depth and extended to incorporate the curriculum and instructional modifications you have identified for your student/s with exceptionalities. A lesson planning pyramid (pages 204 and 205.) focuses on identifying concepts to be taught by asking, "What do I want *all, most* and *some* of the students to learn as a result of the lesson?" (Vaugh, Bos & Schumm, 1997). The form provides areas in which to record lesson format/teaching style, social/physical environment (conditions or lesson location), level of personal assistance and in-class assignments/homework. In addition, there is an agenda, or instructional input, area to specify activities for the lesson. The lesson planning pyramid is designed to stand alone or compliment your existing lesson plans.

*A lesson plan pyramid was developed by Mark's team of teachers. It illustrates how his individual educational goals taken from his IEP "snapshot" and his curriculum modification checklist were incorporated into a lesson plan associated with a specific class period. The teachers involved had clearly delineated their responsibilities. This process precludes potential misunderstandings and facilitates productive teaching partnerships.*

**With thought and effort, all children can learn and grow.**

**Sample Lesson Plan Pyramid**

Date: <u>11-5</u>          Class Period:  <u>9-10:20</u>     Unit/Topic: <u>Language Arts</u>
Lesson Objective(s):
<u>Given designated skill level, student will read, spell, and write words, sentences and</u>
<u>stories emphasizing designated skill area. ( Mark: short vowels)</u>

| Materials | Evaluation |
|---|---|
| Recipe to read charts, Student Journal, Readers, tape recorder, Computer Learning Centers' material. | Daily charts<br><br>Teacher monitor of journal and reading |
| **Delivery** | **Level of Personal Assistance** |
| Teachers as facilitators, Peer tutoring, Cooperative learning groups, learning centers. | Teachers as facilitators, Cooperative group interaction, Peer tutors |
| **Social/Physical Environment** | **In Class/Homework** |
| Group tables<br><br>Learning centers | Learning centers: skill practice<br><br>Home: practice reading |

| Pyramid | Agenda |
|---|---|
| What **some** students will learn — Read, write, spell individual letters and words at designed skill level. | 10 min.  Skill Builders Practice: Peer tutor listens to tutee read sounds or words. Chart.<br><br>15 min.  Each group reviews designated new skills using visuals and music.<br><br>20 min.  Groups write stories incorporating members' different skills. (Mark dictates and illustrates story.) |
| What **most** students will learn — Read, write, spell sentences at designed skill level. | 2 min.  Stretch<br><br>15 min.  Learning centers (choice): Independently or cooperatively in small groups, student/s practice skills, e.g., audio card reader exercises, computer activities, etc. |
| What **all** students will learn — Read, write, spell stories at designed skill level. Write and read original stories; Minimum 5 sentences. | 15 min.  Students read stories.<br><br>2 min.  Assign homework: Read word lists and stories. |

Adapted from Vaughn, S., Bos, C., Schumm, J.S.  (1997).  *Teaching Mainstreamed, Diverse, and At-risk Students*.  Boston: Allyn & Bacon.

# Lesson Plan Pyramid

Date _____  Class_____

Period _____  Unit/Topic _____

Lesson Objective/s _____

_____

_____

| Materials | Evaluation |
|---|---|
| Delivery | Level of Personal Assistance |
| Social/Physical Environment | In Class/Homework |

| Pyramid | Agenda |
|---|---|
| **What some students will learn**<br><br>**What most students will learn**<br><br>**What ALL students will learn** | |

Adapted from Vaughn, S., Bos, C., Schumm, J.S. (1997). *Teaching Mainstreamed, Diverse, and At-risk Students*. Boston: Allyn & Bacon.

## EFFECTIVE INSTRUCTIONAL STRATEGIES

Three instructional strategies have emerged from the literature as being particularly effective when teaching learners with diverse learning characteristics: peer and cross-age tutoring, cooperative learning and flexible grouping.

### *Peer/Cross-Age Tutoring*

Peer and cross-age tutoring operates on the principle that one-on-one instruction will increase students' performance in academic areas and improve students' social skills and behavior more than whole- or small-group instruction. Usually, older students tutor younger students. Both students benefit from the learning experience. Both students benefit academically and socially. Both also become winners when a student with a learning disability tutors a younger student. The exceptional student wins a wealth of self-esteem.

### *Cooperative Learning*

Cooperative learning strategies operates on the age-old principle of social psychology that people working together toward a common goal can achieve more than individuals working separately. Cooperative learning strategies are characterized by a heterogeneous group of students working together, typically in groups of two to six, on lessons assigned by the teacher. They are tested individually, but are rewarded based on the accomplishments of the group as a whole. Cooperative learning has been well documented in research literature as not only improving achievement, but also improving social skills of mixed-ability students, including exceptional students (Slavin, 1991).

### *Flexible Grouping*

Students can be grouped in a number of ways including by interests, skills to be learned, subject proficiency, level of basic skills and prior knowledge. The present trend in general education is toward heterogeneous or mixed-ability grouping, in which students with a wide range of achievement levels are put together for instruction. Since students with different exceptionalities are spending more and more of their school day in general education, they benefit academically and socially from mixed-ability grouping.

*Mark would benefit from participating in any of these instructional groupings, as would most students without exceptionalities. At the elementary level, Mark's teachers involved all their co-taught students in peer tutoring experiences, cooperative learning activities and flexibly grouped learning centers.*

The following pages identify a number of common concerns and offer a variety of simple, yet highly effective, instructional strategies a teacher can use.

**COMMON CONCERNS**

| If a student has difficulty try: | If a student has difficulty try: |
|---|---|
| **Drawing conclusions and making inferences**<br><br>❖ Teaching thinking skills directly<br>❖ Draw a parallel to a situation the student might have prior experience | **Working in groups**<br><br>❖ Provide a partner<br>❖ Provide student with a task or position of leadership<br>❖ Provide more structure by defining tasks and listing steps |
| **Remembering**<br><br>❖ Provide a checklist<br>❖ Provide cues<br>❖ Have students make notes to self<br>❖ Teach memory skills<br>❖ Teach use of acronyms<br>❖ Teach use of mnemonic devices | **Understanding cause/effect; anticipating consequences**<br><br>❖ Use concrete examples<br>❖ Use real-life situations<br>❖ Directly teach cause/effect<br>❖ Brainstorming<br>❖ Role playing<br>❖ Simulation activities |
| **Spelling**<br><br>❖ Dictate word; ask student to repeat it<br>❖ Avoid traditional spelling lists<br>❖ Teach short, easy words in context<br>❖ Have students make flash cards<br>❖ Use spelling patterns or word families<br>❖ Do not penalize for spelling errors<br>❖ Hang words from ceiling or post on walls for constant visual cues<br>❖ Provide a tactile aid to spelling (sandpaper letters, saltbox, etc.) | **Getting started-staying on task**<br><br>❖ Give work in smaller amounts<br>❖ Provide immediate feedback<br>❖ Sequence work<br>❖ Provide time suggestions<br>❖ Check on progress<br>❖ Peer tutor<br>❖ Give cue to begin work |

### Expressing him/herself in writing

- ❖ Accept alternate forms of reporting
  - o oral report
  - o tape-recorded interview
  - o taped interview
  - o maps
  - o photographic essay
  - o panel discussion

- ❖ Student dictates work to others
- ❖ Have student prepare only notes or outline on subject
- ❖ Shorten amount required

### Understanding what is read

- ❖ Reduce the language level
- ❖ Become more concrete
- ❖ Reduce amount of new ideas
- ❖ Provide experiences for a frame of reference
- ❖ Provide study guide
- ❖ Give organizational help
- ❖ Provide alternate media
- ❖ Remove extra words, "Jane, please sit." **not** "Jane would you sit in your chair?"
- ❖ Use fill in the blank technique

### Learning by listening

- ❖ Provide visuals
- ❖ Use flash cards
- ❖ Have student close his eyes and visualize the information
- ❖ Teach use of acronyms
- ❖ Give explanations in small distinct steps
- ❖ Provide study guide

### Paying attention to printed word

- ❖ Select a text at independent level
- ❖ Highlight cues
- ❖ Underline, number
- ❖ Keep desk free of extra materials
- ❖ Use overhead transparencies

### Reading textbooks

- ❖ Use lower level or adaptive text
- ❖ Tape text
- ❖ Shorten amount of required reading
- ❖ Have students read aloud in small groups
- ❖ Allow extra time for reading
- ❖ Omit reading requirements
- ❖ Put main ideas on index cards
- ❖ Use a buddy or a work group
- ❖ Pre-teach vocabulary

### Expressing him/herself verbally

- ❖ Accept alternative forms of repeating
  - o written report
  - o artwork or exhibit
  - o chart/graph
  - o bulletin board
  - o photos
- ❖ Ask questions requiring short answers
- ❖ Provide prompts
- ❖ Give rules for class discussion
- ❖ Let student speak in smaller groups
- ❖ Allow taped reports

**Notes:**

**When parents and teachers work together, the student benefits.**

**Section C**

# RESOURCES: WHO? WHERE? WHAT?

## PARENTS AND/OR GUARDIANS

Parents are invaluable resources of information helpful to their child's academic, social and emotional development. It is especially important to communicate regularly and candidly with parents of students with varied exceptionalities. Parents are the people who will follow through with reality-based instruction in their home and community.

There are many ways to communicate with parents: phone calls, FAX messages, e-mail, letters, newsletters, networking through other parents, notes sent home with their children, written progress notices, phone calls reminding parents of upcoming meetings, invitations to visit or to help out at school and home visits. (Refer to Chapters 4 and 5.) Parents of students with an exceptionality most often want to know how well their child is progressing academically and behaviorally with their goals (Turnball & Turnball, 1997). It is important to frequently report positive progress to parents, thereby, developing rapport.

## SCHOOL OR DISTRICT PERSONNEL

There are several professionals who are considered support personnel who will also assist your efforts. Not every school or school district will employ all the personnel listed. However, some assistance will be available within any given school or district. Support personnel include:

- ❖ Special education teachers
- ❖ Reading and Title 1 teachers
- ❖ School psychologists
- ❖ Counselors
- ❖ School staff
- ❖ Social workers
- ❖ Nurses

- ❖ ESL teachers
- ❖ Speech or language specialists
- ❖ Physical and occupational therapists
- ❖ Vocational teachers and coordinators
- ❖ Specialists for the hearing or visually impaired
- ❖ Media specialists

*Mark was supported by a special education teacher who co-taught with the regular second grade teacher during language arts.*

211

## EDUCATIONAL SUPPORT TEAMS

Educational support teams have been implemented in many school systems to help you solve instructional and social/behavior problems. Using a number of different names, including building assistance team or school-wide assistance team, the team typically consists of four educators, elected by their peers, who provide assistance to teachers in meeting the needs of all students in their classrooms. *Project RIDE* is an example of a program incorporating a School-Wide Assistance Team which targets specific problems that students are experiencing and helps teachers establish effective instructional and/or behavioral strategies for all children to be successful.

*Project RIDE* provides early childhood, elementary and middle school teachers with the skills, resources and support necessary to accommodate at-risk students within the regular classroom. *RIDE* is a building-based support system which operates on the premise that teachers, when coupled with proven classroom practices and modern technology, can become their own best resource. The project supports the belief that every student belongs to the educational family and should be considered the responsibility of the entire building staff. In keeping with its holistic approach, *RIDE* seeks to accommodate the needs of most atypical learners in the regular classroom setting.

There are three major components of RIDE:

1. **Effective Classroom Practices**

   Over 70 classroom practices drawn from the "effective schools" literature were translated into question/answer format and included in *RIDE*. Teachers are asked to compare "what should be" versus "what is" within their respective classrooms.

2. **Computer Tactics Bank and Video Library**

   The user-friendly Computer Tactics Bank (Apple, IBM or Mac format) contains over 500 proven tactics selected from the literature. The tactics address over 35 at-risk behaviors that were identified by teachers as causing problems within their classrooms. The Video Library includes 80 color video demonstrations of how to carry out the proven academic and social tactics.

3. **School-Wide Assistance Team (SWAT)**

   Based on the premise that teachers are often their own best resource, the SWAT process encourages a building-level team of teachers to address problems encountered by their peers. Through the SWAT process, the experience and repertoires of experienced practitioners are collectively and systematically used to help teachers deal with academic and behavioral problems within their classrooms.

   This project has been approved by the U.S. Department of Education, National Diffusion Network as a validated project for at-risk elementary students.

(For further information, please contact: Dr. Ray Beck, Project Director, Sopris West, Inc., P.O. Box 1809, Longmont, CO 80502-1809, (303) 651-2829.)

# GLOSSARY

**Advocacy.** One of the primary characteristics of the Individuals with Disabilities Education Act, which involves the assignment of representatives (advocates) for individuals with disabilities who lack parents or guardians.

**Articulation disorders.** Occur when students are unable to produce the sounds and sound combinations of language.

**Attention Deficit Disorder (ADD).** A disorder consisting of two subtypes of behavior; inattention and hyperactivity-impulsivity.

**Audiogram.** A visual representation of an individual's ability to hear sound.

**Autism.** A developmental disability characterized by extreme withdrawal and communication difficulties.

**Blind.** Describes an individual who is unable to see and therefore, uses tactual (touch) and auditory (hearing) abilities to access the environment.

**Cerebral palsy.** Results from damage to the brain before or during birth; conditions are classified according to the areas affected and the types of symptoms.

**Child Find.** A requirement that each state identify and track the number of students with disabilities and plan for their educational needs.

**Classwide Peer Tutoring.** Students of different reading levels (one average or high, and one low) are paired and read materials that can be easily read by the least able reader in the pair.

**Collaboration.** A style for direct interaction between at least two co-equal parties voluntarily engaged in shared decision making as they work toward a common goal.

**Compensatory education.** Instruction designed to compensate (make up) for prior lack of educational opportunities, and intervention or prevention programs.

**Consultation model.** An interactive process that enables people with diverse expertise to generate creative solutions to mutually defined problems.

**Continuum of services.** A full range of service options for students with disabilities, provided by the school system.

**Cooperative learning groups.** Groups of students work together toward a common goal, usually to help one another learn academic material.

**Cooperative teaching.** General and special education teachers work together to coordinate curriculum and instruction and teach heterogeneous groups of students in the general education classroom setting.

**Co-planning.** General and special education teachers work together to plan activities for students.

**Creatively gifted or talented.** Describes students who display their unique abilities within the framework of various forms of communication (drawing, music, singing, writing and acting).

**Cross-age pairing.** A method of pairing older students with younger students for reading instruction.

**Cross-categorical approach.** Accommodations for exceptional learners are discussed in terms of students' shared needs rather than in terms of their identification as members of a disability category.

**Deaf.** Describes a person with a severe or profound loss of hearing.

**Deafness-blindness.** Also known as *dual sensory impairment*; involves impairments in the two main channels (auditory and visual) of receptive communication and learning.

**Down Syndrome.** One of the most common chromosomal disorders, usually associated with mental retardation.

**Due process.** Ensures that everyone with a stake in the student's educational success has a voice; also addresses written notification to parents for referral and testing for special education, parental consent, and guidelines for appeals and record keeping, education classrooms, resource rooms, special schools and other types of settings.

**Educational placement.** The type of educational setting in which a particular student is instructed; examples include general education classrooms, resource rooms, special schools and other types of settings.

**Emotional or behavioral disorders.** Behavior that falls considerably outside the norm.

**Enrichment.** Adding breadth and depth to the traditional curriculum.

**Epilepsy.** A condition characterized by the tendency to have recurrent seizures that are sudden, excessive, spontaneous and abnormal discharges of neurons accompanied by alteration in motor function, and/or sensory function and/or consciousness.

**Equity pedagogy.** The teacher attends to different teaching and learning styles and modifies teaching to facilitate the academic achievement for students from diverse cultures.

**Exceptionalities.** Refers to students who represent a range of disability categories (e.g., students with emotional disorders, learning disabilities, physical impairments and students who are gifted).

**Fetal Alcohol Syndrome (FAS).** Refers to a spectrum of birth defects caused by the mother drinking during pregnancy.

**Flexible grouping.** The use of different student patterns that vary in composition, size and frequency of meetings.

**Free and Appropriate Public Education (FAPE).** Mandatory legislation provides that all children with disabilities be given a free and appropriate public education.

**Full inclusion.** A movement that advocates educating all students with disabilities in the general education classroom full-time.

**Giftedness.** Evidence of high performance capability in areas such as intelligence, creativity, art, or leadership, or in specific academic fields, that requires services or activities not ordinarily provided by the school in order to more fully develop these capabilities.

**Hard of hearing.** Describes a person with a mild to moderate loss of hearing.

**Hyperactivity.** Refers to a group of behaviors associated with restlessness and excess motor activity.

**Inclusion.** The situation in which students with disabilities are educated with their non-disabled peers, with special education supports and services provided as needed.

**Inclusion support teachers.** A teacher whose responsibilities include supporting students with disabilities (e.g., mental retardation, severe disabilities, physical disabilities, visual impairments) in general education classrooms.

**Individualized Education Program (IEP).** A written plan, developed to meet the special learning needs of each student with disabilities.

**Individuals with Disabilities Education (IDEA).** Legislation designed to ensure that all children with disabilities receive an appropriate education through special education and related services.

**Interactive planning.** Involves monitoring students' learning and making adaptations in response to their needs.

**Learning Disability.** A condition present in children with average or above average potential intelligence who are experiencing a severe discrepancy between their ability and achievement in specific areas: reading, writing, spelling, language or math.

**Least Restrictive Environment (LRE).** The instructional setting most like that of non-disabled peers that also meets the educational needs of each student with disabilities.

**Legal blindness.** Describes an individual who with the best possible correction in the better eye has a measured visual acuity of 20/200 or worse, or a visual field restricted to 20 degrees or less.

**Lesson Planning Pyramid.** A framework for lesson planning that helps teachers consider individual student needs within the context of planning for the class as a whole.

**Mainstreaming.** The participation of students with disabilities in general education classrooms to the extent appropriate for meeting their needs.

**Mental retardation.** Characterize individuals who have limited intellectual functioning that affects their learning.

**Multidisciplinary Team (MDT).** This group of individuals usually includes a representative of the local education agency, the classroom teacher, the special education teacher, parents or guardians and, when appropriate, the student, who together develop and implement the IEP.

**Multiple disabilities.** Describes individuals who have severe or profound mental retardation and one or more significant motor or sensory impairments and/or special health needs.

**Multiple intelligences.** Theory that human beings are capable of exhibiting intelligence in seven domains: linguistic, logical-mathematical, spatial, musical, bodily-kinesthetic, interpersonal (i.e., discerning and responding to the needs of others), and intrapersonal (i.e., having detailed and accurate self-knowledge).

**Muscular Dystrophy (MD).** A chronic disorder characterized by the weakening and wasting of the body's muscles.

**Noncompliance.** Failure to comply with the law; the Individuals with Disabilities Act requires that states mandate consequences for noncompliance.

**Orthopedic impairment.** Includes deficits caused by congenital anomaly (e.g., clubfoot, absence of some member), impairments caused by disease (e.g., poliomyelitis, bone tuberculosis) and impairments from other causes (e.g., cerebral palsy, amputation, and fractures or burns that cause contractures).

**Other Health Impairments (OHI).** Limited strength, vitality, or alertness (caused by chronic or acute health problems such as heart condition, tuberculosis, rheumatic fever, nephritis, asthma, sickle cell anemia, hemophilia, epilepsy, lead poisoning, leukemia or diabetes) that adversely affects a student's educational performance.

**Partial participation.** A concept that assumes an individual has the right to participate, to the extent possible, in all activities.

**Partially sighted.** Describes an individual who with best possible correction in the better eye has a measured visual acuity between 20/70 and 20/200.

**Peer Collaboration Model.** Developed to help classroom teachers solve problems by providing time and structure to do so.

**Peer tutoring.** One student in a pair acts as a teacher for the other student.

**Prereferral Assistance Team (PAT).** A group of teachers from the same school who meet regularly to discuss the specific progress of students brought to their attention by other teachers in the school.

**Neurological impairment.** A disability caused by a dysfunction of the brain, spinal cord, and nerves, thereby creating transmission of improper instruction, uncontrolled bursts of instructions from the brain, or incorrect interpretation of feedback to the brain.

*Trade Secrets*

**Public Law 94-142.** This legislation, designed to ensure that all children with disabilities receive an appropriate education through special education and related services, was originally referred to as the Education for All Handicapped Children Act, enacted in 1975, and later reauthorized and expanded as the Individuals with Disabilities Education Act (IDEA).

**Pull-out Program.** Programs in which children are literally pulled out of their general education classroom for supplemental instruction in basic skills.

**Regular Education Initiative (REI).** A concept that promotes coordination of services between regular and special education.

**Related services.** The types of services to which students with disabilities are entitled, including: speech therapy, ideology, psychological services, physical therapy, occupational therapy, recreation, early identification and assessment, counseling, medical services for diagnostic or evaluation purposes, school health services, transportation and social work services.

**Remediation.** Additional instruction for students who do not demonstrate, at an expected rate, competency, in basic skills in reading, writing and mathematics.

**Special education resource room.** A placement outside the general education classroom where students with disabilities receive specialized, individualized, and intensive instruction to meet their needs.

**Specific learning disabilities.** Represents a heterogeneous group of students who, despite adequate cognitive functioning and the ability to learn some skills and strategies quickly and easily, have great difficulty learning other skills and strategies.

**Speech disorders.** Disorders that involve unintelligible or unpleasant communication.

**Spina bifida.** A birth defect that occurs when the spinal cord fails to close properly.

**Students at risk.** Students who fail to succeed academically and who require additional instruction.

**Systems of support.** Refers to the coordinated set of services and accommodations matched to the student's needs.

**Teacher Assistance Team (TAT).** A group of teachers who provide initial strategies and support for fellow classroom teachers prior to referring a student for assessment for special education services.

**Transdisciplinary teaming.** Refers to a group of experts working together and viewing the students as a whole instead of working independently in a single specialty area.

**Traumatic brain injury.** An injury to the brain, caused by an external physical force, that causes total or partial functional disability or psychosocial impairment, or both, which adversely affects a student's educational performance.

**Tutoring.** A systematic plan for supplementing the student's educational program.

**Visual acuity.** The clarity with which an individual can see an object from a distance of 20 feet.

**Vocational Rehabilitation Act.** This act (Public Law 93-112) prevents any private organization that uses federal funds, or any local or state disabilities solely on the basis of those disabilities.

**Zero reject.** An element of IDEA that states no child with disabilities can be excluded from receiving a free and appropriate education.

Adapted from Vaughn, S., Boos, C., Schumn, J.S. (1977). Teaching Mainstreamed, Diverse, and At-Risk Students. Boston, Allyn, & Bacon.

## CHAPTER CHECKLIST

Do you know the answers to the following questions?

Yes    No

☐    ☐    What is special education?

☐    ☐    Where does special education happen?

☐    ☐    What types of exceptionalities are there?

☐    ☐    What causes some of these exceptionalities?

☐    ☐    What should you do if you suspect a student may need special education services?

☐    ☐    What is a formal referral and identification process for special education?

☐    ☐    What is an Individualized Education Program (IEP)?

☐    ☐    What roles should you, your students and their parents play in the development and implementation of IEPs?

☐    ☐    What information should you, the classroom teacher, receive about a student with an exceptionality in your class?

☐    ☐    How are special educational supports provided?

☐    ☐    What is the model at your school?

☐    ☐    How can you modify curriculum and instruction?

☐    ☐    What are some effective instructional strategies you can use?

☐    ☐    How can curriculum and instructional modifications be incorporated into your daily schedule?

☐    ☐    How can curriculum and instructional modifications be incorporated into your regular lesson plans?

☐    ☐    Who, where and what are some valuable resources?

*Trade Secrets*

**Notes:**

218

Chapter 7

# TEACHING LANGUAGE – MINORITY STUDENTS

**Section A:** **Myths about Second Language Learning**

**Section B:** **Program Models**

**Section C:** **Language Learning Principles**
- ❖ Positive Attitudes Toward the Second Language Learner
- ❖ Strategies That Support Second Language Learners

**Section D:** **Strategies for Content Area Teachers**
- ❖ Clarifying Concepts
- ❖ Reading Strategies
- ❖ Feeling Successful
- ❖ Check for Understanding

**Section E:** **Involving Parents**

**Chapter Checklist**

The number of Limited English Proficient (LEP) students in the United States is rapidly rising. Between 1985 and 1992, the number of LEP students enrolled in U.S. schools increased by nearly 70 percent. This is two and one half times faster than the general school enrollment. It totals more than 2.5 million students, according to the group Teachers of English to Speakers of Other Languages (TESOL). During the same period, LEP students increased from 3.8 percent to slightly more than 6 percent of the total K-12 student population, and that proportion continues to expand (Willis, ASCD Update). About one in seven of the nation's school-age youth speaks a home language other than English, and the number of such young people is growing. Spanish speakers represent the majority of LEP students (75%), followed by speakers of Asian languages (12%) and other languages.

Because of these statistics, it is very probable that you will teach in a classroom where at least some of the students are learning English as a second language. Research on second language learning has shown that there are many misconceptions about how children learn languages. Teachers need to be aware of these research findings and unlearn old ways of thinking. Language learning by school-aged children takes longer, is harder and involves a great deal more struggle than most teachers have been led to believe. In order to successfully teach these students, it is important to first dispel some of the common myths regarding second language learning.

 Children easily learn two or even more languages that are spoken in their home environment during the first 48 months of their life. After age four, a child's ability to quickly learn a second language is greatly reduced.

## Section A

## MYTHS ABOUT SECOND LANGUAGE LEARNING

*Myth 1:*  *ESL students learn English easily and quickly simply by being exposed to and surrounded by native-English speakers.*

**Fact:**  After age three, a second language takes time and significant intellectual effort on the part of the learner.  Learning a second language is hard work; learners do not simply pick up the language.

*Myth 2:*  *When ESL learners are able to converse comfortably in English, they have developed proficiency in the language.*

**Fact:**  Research has shown that it can take six to nine years for ESL students to achieve the same levels of proficiency in academic English as native speakers.

*Myth 3:*  *Any amount of native-language content instruction is detrimental for students who are non or limited-English proficient.*

**Fact:**  LEP students who receive no instruction in their native language often develop a negative self-concept, are retained and ultimately may drop out of school.  There is a great deal of evidence that oral communication skills in a second language may be acquired within two or three years. But it may take up to four to six years to acquire the level of proficiency for understanding the language in its instructional uses (Collier, 1989; Cummins, 1981).

*Myth 4:*  *In earlier times, immigrant children learned English rapidly and assimilated easily into American life.*

**Fact:**  Many immigrant students during the early part of this century did not learn English quickly or well.  Many dropped out of school to work in jobs that did not require the kinds of academic achievement and communication skills that substantive employment opportunities require today.

According to researcher Virginia Collier of George Mason University, the more native-language instructional support LEP students receive, the more they are able to achieve in English in each succeeding academic year. Students who do not receive native-language instruction appear to do well in the early grades, but their performance fails to match that of the norm group. Their gains go down as they reach upper elementary and secondary schooling. This is due to the fact that students' cognitive academic language proficiency does not match their basic interpersonal communication skills.

*There are virtually dozens of unique languages spoken in classrooms today.*

**Section B**

## PROGRAM MODELS

English as a Second Language (ESL) programs (rather than bilingual programs) are likely to be used in districts where the language minority population is very diverse and represents many different languages. ESL programs can accommodate students from different language backgrounds in the same class, and teachers do not need to be proficient in the native language of their students.

No matter what the situation or type of program in which you find yourself working, it's important to remember that acquiring a new language is a complex task that requires the intellectual and emotional involvement of both student and teacher. It can be an exciting and rewarding experience for both. The following describes a number of different ESL program models that exist in various school districts depending upon the population and student needs.

**ESL Pull-Out -** is generally used in elementary school settings. Students spend part of the school day in a mainstream classroom, but are pulled out for a portion of each day to receive instruction in English as a second language. Although schools with a large number of ESL students may have a full-time ESL teacher, some districts employ an ESL teacher who travels to several schools to work with small groups of students scattered throughout the district. If any students in your class are pulled out for ESL instruction, it is imperative that you communicate with the ESL teacher and tell her what content instruction the ESL students are missing. It is also important that you share with the ESL teacher any difficulties that the limited English proficient students are having in the regular classroom.

```
┌─────────────────┐
│                 │
│  Regular Class  │ ──────────▶    ( ESL )
│                 │
└─────────────────┘
```

**ESL Class Period -** is generally used in middle and secondary school settings. Students receive ESL instruction during a regular class period and usually receive course credit. They may be grouped for instruction according to their level of English proficiency.

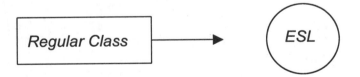

```
┌────────┐       ┌────────┐              ┌────────┐
│ Class  │   +   │ Class  │   +  ( ESL ) +  │ Class  │
└────────┘       └────────┘              └────────┘
```

**ESL Resource Center -** is a variation of the pull-out design, bringing students together from several classrooms or schools. The resource center concentrates ESL materials and staff in one location and is usually staffed by at least one full-time ESL teacher.

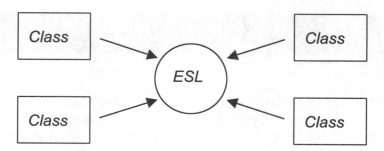

**Sheltered English/Content-based Programs -** group language minority students from different language backgrounds together in classes where teachers use English as the medium for providing content area instruction, adapting their language to the proficiency level of the students. They may also use gestures and visual aids to help the students understand. Although the acquisition of English is one of the goals of sheltered English and content-based programs, instruction focuses on content rather than language.

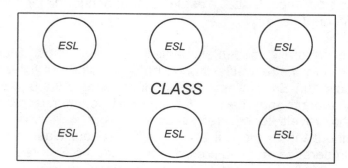

**Structured Immersion Programs -** use only English, but there is no explicit ESL instruction. As in sheltered English and content-based programs, English is taught through the content areas. Structured immersion teachers have strong content area knowledge, good receptive skills in their students' first language, and a bilingual education or ESL endorsement. The teacher's use of the student's first language is limited primarily to clarification of English instruction.

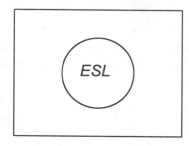

**Section C**

# LANGUAGE LEARNING PRINCIPLES

The following section offers two major themes regarding second language learning. The first deals with building positive attitudes toward the second language learner and the second describes strategies that support second language learners.

## POSITIVE ATTITUDES TOWARD THE SECOND LANGUAGE LEARNER

**Have high expectations -** Children are natural acquirers of language. Expect them to become proficient in English. Many students have already acquired a first language successfully. All concepts and skills learned in their native language can easily be transferred to the second language.

**Remember that language is a process -** Second language learners start out in the silent stage, which may last from one day to a few months. They should not be forced to speak during this time but can follow comprehensible directions and listen to comprehensible stories, nursery rhymes and songs. They will usually understand much more than they can express.

**Take time to develop good rapport with your students -** Students who have positive feelings about English and the people who speak English are more highly motivated to learn the language. Ask your students how to pronounce their names. Your ESL students will appreciate the respect and courtesy your efforts show. Try to learn something about the students' cultural backgrounds, which may make you more sensitive to unfamiliar behavior or responses.

**Set a cheerful tone of confidence in the classroom -** Students cannot learn effectively when they are anxious and upset. Acknowledge any evidence of learning. Take time to establish a supportive environment.

**Find ways that all learners can experience success with language in context -** Students learn at different rates. Language aptitude, age, personality and cultural and linguistic background all affect the rate and proficiency of language learning. Use gestures, facial expressions, demonstrations and tone of voice to help students understand the message you are trying to convey. Bring in real objects and other visuals. Provide real-life, hands-on experiences for the students. Second language learners take things very literally; so always check for understanding by asking specific questions.

225

## STRATEGIES THAT SUPPORT SECOND LANGUAGE LEARNERS

**Teach language as it is really used** - Don't worry about such things as subjunctive or the difference between who and whom. Even native speakers misuse these, but are easily understood. You can help ESL learners by using cognates whenever possible and basic words that have broad meanings.

### COGNATES

| Spanish | English |
|---|---|
| honor | honor |
| real | real |
| negro | black |
| tres | trio |
| pantalones | pants |
| rodeo | rodeo |
| jardin | garden |
| carro | car |
| color | color |

**Let grammar emerge from the communication goal** - Teach grammar as it is needed for successful communication. Try not to teach it in isolation or for its own sake.

**Don't get discouraged by errors** - An error does not necessarily mean that the student has not learned a particular language feature. There is usually a lag between understanding a particular language feature and the student's ability to use it.

**Adapt your language to the ability of your students** - Although sentences should be grammatically correct, you can simplify structures, slow the pace, limit your vocabulary, speak clearly and control the use of obscure idioms. But keep the language natural. You may need to pause longer where you would normally pause in speaking or say important sentences in several different ways.

**Accept language interference** - Accented speech and some grammatical errors are inevitable for second language learners and are acceptable as long as students can communicate effectively. The new language has been superimposed on an existing system; there is bound to be interference between the two.

**Keep the class student-centered** - Develop opportunities for students to learn English by using it. Students should be talking while the teacher acts as a language guide.

**Make language learning incidental to some other task** – Do not spend an inordinate amount of time with drill and practice or learning vocabulary in isolation. Teach students important concepts and the vocabulary for those concepts the other students are learning.

**Have students help each other learn -** Language is social. Second language learners must have numerous opportunities for interacting with peers, especially proficient English speakers. Use cooperative learning, a buddy system, peer tutoring, or some other means to enable the more fluent students to help those who are non-native speakers of English. Use student pairs for team learning, especially for reports, experiments, and projects.

**Vary classroom activities -** Plan lessons in short segments and allow students to be actively engaged throughout the lesson. Develop thematic units to cover concepts and vocabulary in interesting, meaningful ways. Use children's literature, guests, and hands-on experiences to teach concepts and vocabulary. When having students practice, remember that massed practice promotes fast learning and distributed practice promotes lasting learning. If you want students to remember something for a long time, it must be practiced over and over again, gradually lengthening the amount of time between practice sessions.

***A dramatic play center -*** A dramatic play center for primary children can mimic the home environment. Boxes of food, coupons, labels for utensils and dishes, pictures, and miniature appliances enable students to use their second language in a non-threatening situation. Teachers have found that students break their "silent period" more quickly during this type of pretend play.

**Singing -** Singing in the chorus gives the ESL child a chance to learn to pronounce strange new words in a risk-free activity. Bonus: If the English songs are displayed on a chart and the teacher points to each word as it is sung, children receive an easy "reading" lesson.

*When students work together they share language, everyday concepts and friendships.*

*Trade Secrets*

## Notes:

228

## STRATEGIES FOR CONTENT AREA TEACHERS

If you are a content area teacher with limited English proficient students in your class, there are many strategies you can use to enable your ESL students to master the same concepts that your native English speakers do.

Too often one hears of the problems of cultural and linguistic diversity in our country's schools rather than the opportunity that diversity provides. Students from other countries and cultures enrich our schools and enable our students to grow in many important ways. Student diversity may challenge our educational system, but the educational innovations and instructional strategies that are effective with diverse students can benefit all students. Some of these common questions and effective strategies can be explained in the following letters between ESL resource teachers and concerned classroom teachers.

*Teachers need to clarify concepts immediately.*

## CLARIFYING CONCEPTS

*Dear ESL Resource Teacher,*

The ESL students in my classroom seem to be doing fine with conversational English. They communicate very well on the playground, know English greetings, farewell, numbers, colors and basic phrases. However, they seem to have difficulty grasping concepts with technical vocabulary and unfamiliar language. How can I help them acquire these important concepts that the other students are learning?

*Signed, Concerned Teacher.*

*Dear Concerned Teacher,*

Your question is a very good one and shows your sincere desire for all students to learn. The situation you describe is very common and can be dealt with in several ways.

❖ Explain special vocabulary terms in words known to the students.

❖ Provide clear illustrations and concrete examples to assist students in understanding new words, complex concepts and skills. Choose visuals that are not cluttered and synchronize your gestures with your words as you focus on different parts of a picture.

❖ Use pictures, tables, maps, diagrams, globes, and other visual aids to assist in comparison and contrast for comprehension of concepts. Show the same information through a variety of different charts and visuals.

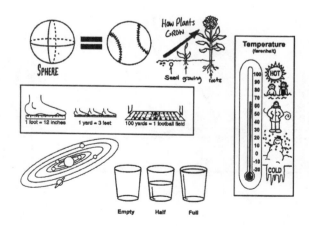

*Visual aids support comprehension.*

## READING STRATEGIES

*Dear ESL Resource Teacher,*

How can I best support reading instruction for my ESL students? I know they need extra help in order to improve their reading skills, but I am not sure what methods or materials I should use. Can you help?

*Signed, Concerned Teacher.*

*Dear Concerned Teacher,*

There are several simple ways to support reading instruction for your ESL students. Since they probably are hearing and speaking the new language for the first time, they need additional practice listening to the second language. They will also need extra help with the books they are reading. Try these ideas:

- ❖ Support reading instruction by providing CD ROMs, videos, audiocassettes, and other materials that may be used independently or in small groups.

- ❖ Prepare difficult passages from textbooks on tape for listening.

- ❖ Maintain a library of supplementary books written in simple English that offer additional illustrations for problem areas.

- ❖ Highlight written materials for readability by enlarging the size of print, organizing chapters meaningfully and highlighting the headings that show introductions for transition from one idea to another.

Other ways to increase motivation, aid in retention and keep students on task are:

- ❖ Make material interesting and meaningful.

- ❖ Provide biographies of significant men and women from different cultures.

- ❖ Develop interest and arouse curiosity through hands-on experiences, the out-of-doors and simulations.

- ❖ Offer a variety of reference materials at the students' instructional level for independent use.

- ❖ Collect many of the comic books available that portray historic and cultural events in simplified language.

## FEELING SUCCESSFUL

*Dear ESL Teacher,*

How can I help ESL students experience success in my classroom?

*Signed, Concerned Teacher.*

*Dear Concerned Teacher,*

While students are learning a new language, they still need opportunities to be recognized and feel successful.  Here are a few suggestions.

❖ Tape-record problems for independent listening assignments.

❖ Write instructions and problems that must be worked.  If directions are written, ESL students can read the directions more than once, refer to them and show them to others who may be helping.

❖ Limit the number of problems that must be worked, the number of variables in lab experiments, or the number of questions to be answered.  Consider allowing the students to give an oral report rather than a written one to demonstrate comprehension more accurately.

❖ De-emphasize speed and emphasize accuracy of work.  Second language learners need more time to process and produce their second language.  They may need more time for a test, test questions in their native language, drawings, charts, and gestures until they have adequate second language acquisition.

❖ Teach selectively. Be clear about what is important; teach to the objective. Separate important points from periphery information.

❖ Include frequent checks for comprehension. Dialogue between you and your students can alert you to avoid confusion and misunderstanding. Ask a question that requires all students to demonstrate their understanding of a concept.  This practice will also force students to stay on task and be involved in their learning.

❖ Allow for multiple ways to demonstrate their comprehension.  Oral language is just one form of expression.  ESL students can also demonstrate their understanding of concepts through artistic expression.

# CHECK FOR UNDERSTANDING

*Dear ESL Teacher,*

How do I know that my ESL students have really understood the concepts that have been presented?

*Signed, Concerned Teacher*

*Dear Concerned Teacher,*

You asked an important question. Nodding heads and shy smiles do not always mean a student comprehends. Here are a few ways to check for understanding.

❖ An inexpensive way for a visual check for understanding is to laminate white paper, distribute transparency pens for students to write on the paper and hold up their answers; wipe off with tissue, and collect pens at the end of the lesson or class.

❖ Make squares of red and green construction paper for students to hold up to indicate their responses. Red is for "no" or "false." Green is for "yes" or "true."

❖ Have students jot down their responses on sticky notes that they put on the side of their desk. The teacher can circulate around the class and check answers.

❖ At the end of a class or lesson, tell students to summarize what they have learned. This summarization will be their "ticket out of class."

❖ Use signals as often as possible. This allows the teacher to check for understanding from all of the students simultaneously. For instance, when checking students' understanding of sequencing, have them hold up one finger if the incident happens first, two fingers if it occurs second, and three fingers if what you are describing happens third in a sequence.

# Notes:

## Section E

### INVOLVING PARENTS

One of the most challenging problems you will face is how to interact with and involve parents of ESL learners. This is a complicated situation that requires patience, understanding, and a sincere desire to learn about another culture and community. You will need to learn about the home environment of your students while their parents learn about school-oriented activities and programs. In order to build bridges between the home and the school, try to keep the following suggestions in mind:

1. Learn to pronounce the child's first and last name correctly. This will show how much you value their son or daughter.

2. Make your classroom a friendly place for parents of students from all cultures by including bulletin boards, class work and proverbs from around the world.

***Teachers need to reach out to language-minority parents.***

3. Have an ESL resource teacher, bilingual teacher, or bilingual aide review the information you are sending to parents.

4. Learn a few words or phrases in the first language of your ESL students, for example: Bon Jour, Hola!, Guten Tag or Bon Dia.

5.  Allow your students to translate for their parents at conference and open houses. Tell the parents how much you enjoy teaching their children and encourage them to attend school functions and help in the classroom.

6.  Use bilingual parents to translate for those parents who have not yet mastered English sufficiently to communicate with you.

7.  Investigate the possibility of having an adult ESL class taught on your campus. This would help familiarize the parents with your campus and show them that we are all learning new skills.

8.  Ask your principal to create a welcome room for parents of all students at your school. Have coffee, tea, juice, cookies, or some sort of refreshment in this room on a regular basis. Ask parents to bring their favorite recipes to exchange with others. Have information about the school, classes and parent participation in several languages. Invite the school nurse to stop by and tell parents about immunizations and wellness checks.

9.  Have parents who have served as parent volunteers accompany first-time visitors to the classroom.

10. Invite parents to "show-and-tell." They may have interesting artifacts that their child can describe or which can be understood with very little language.

11. Have a potluck dinner, the main purpose being to bring parents on campus and make them feel comfortable with you and one another. Walk around and shake hands, smile and thank them for attending. Have students perform at this event. Few parents will miss the opportunity to see their children demonstrate their talents.

12. Have babysitting available at functions so that parents can bring their other children and not have to worry about hiring a babysitter. This will make it much more convenient for them and increase the likelihood that they will attend.

13. Videotape a teacher involved in storybook reading in English or in the student's native language. Allow students to take copies of the tape home so that parents can view it and begin to develop the habit of reading as a bedtime ritual.

236

**CHAPTER CHECKLIST:**

Yes   No

☐   ☐
☐   ☐

Myths - I understand how:
Second languages are learned.
Myths distort effective ESL instruction.

☐   ☐

☐   ☐

Program Models - I understand:
The difference between the five most commonly used ESL programs.
What approach my school uses.

☐   ☐
☐   ☐

Language Learning Principles- I know:
What attitudes support second language learning.
A number of effective ESL strategies.

☐   ☐
☐   ☐

☐   ☐
☐   ☐

Strategies for Content Area Teachers - I know how:
To clarify concepts for ESL students.
To use effective content reading strategies for ESL students.
To help my ESL students feel successful.
To check ESL students' understanding of new concepts.

☐   ☐
☐   ☐

Involving Parents - I know how:
To communicate with language-minority parents.
To help language-minority parents feel comfortable in communicating with me.

# Notes:

Chapter 8

# STRESS MANAGEMENT:
# HOW TO BALANCE THE ACT

*Learning how to balance your personal and professional life is essential.*

**Section A**

# BALANCING THE LIFE OF A TEACHER

Research has shown that teachers enter the field with anticipation of their career and the impact they will have on students. The complexity of teaching soon becomes a reality. The workload increases and the demands are endless. Physical well-being is a concern. Teachers must be intentional about managing themselves professionally to balance their responsibilities for teacher and student success.

*Stress occurs when our fantasies and our realities are far apart.*

Effective teachers have been able to manage and balance their professional lives. They have even been able to create a balance with their life apart from school. This chapter addresses ways to proactively manage your time and stress in your personal and professional life.

241

**NOTES:**

## Section B

# TO STRESS OR NOT TO STRESS

| ARRAY INTERACTION INVENTORY |
|---|

Complete the following survey to help identify your primary and secondary personal objectives, the most natural ways you respond to the world.

Directions:

- Rank order the responses in rows below on a scale from 1 to 4 with:

    **1 being "least like me"** to **4 being "most like me."**

- After you have ranked each row, add down each column.

- The column/s with the highest score/s shows your primary Personal Objective/s.

**In your normal day-to-day life, you tend to be:**

| Nurturing Sensitive Caring | | Logical Systematic Organized | | Spontaneous Creative Playful | | Quiet Insightful Reflective | |
|---|---|---|---|---|---|---|---|

**In your normal day-to-day life, you tend to value:**

| Harmony Relationships | | Work Time schedules | | Stimulation Having fun | | Reflection Having some time alone | |
|---|---|---|---|---|---|---|---|

**In most settings, you are usually:**

| Authentic Compassionate Harmonious | | Traditional Responsible Parental | | Active Opportunistic Spontaneous | | Inventive Competent Seeking | |
|---|---|---|---|---|---|---|---|

**In most situations, you could be described as:**

| Empathetic Communicative Devoted | | Practical Competitive Loyal | | Impetuous Impactful Daring | | Conceptual Knowledgeable Composed | |
|---|---|---|---|---|---|---|---|

**You approach most tasks in a(n) _____ manner.**

| Affectionate Inspirational Vivacious | | Conventional Orderly Concerned | | Courageous Adventurous Impulsive | | Rational Philosophical Complex | |
|---|---|---|---|---|---|---|---|

**When things start to "not go your way" and you are tired and worn down, what might your responses be?**

| Say "I'm sorry" Make mistakes Feel badly | | Over-control Become critical Take charge | | "It's not my fault" Manipulate Act out | | Withdraw Not talk Indecisive | |
|---|---|---|---|---|---|---|---|

**When you've "had-a-bad-day" and you become frustrated, how might you respond?**

| Over-please Cry Feel depressed | | Be perfectionistic Verbally attack Overwork | | Become physical Be irresponsible Demand attention | | Disengage Delay Daydream | |
|---|---|---|---|---|---|---|---|

| Add score: | | | | | | | |
|---|---|---|---|---|---|---|---|
| **Harmony** | | **Production** | | **Connection** | | **Status Quo** | |

©Kortman, 1997

243

## THE ARRAY MODEL - WHO AM I?

The Array Interaction Inventory is based upon the Array Model (Knaupp, 1995), which identifies four personality components called "Personal Objectives." Every person has all four components within their personality composition; however, one component usually tends to dominate the way a person perceives/responds to life. The following graph describes how each personality component/personal objective responds in both a positive (cooperative) state and a stress (reluctant) state. You may recognize qualities of your own personality for both your primary and secondary personal objectives.

### *Personal Objective/Personality Components*

|  | HARMONY | PRODUCTION | CONNECTION | STATUS QUO |
|---|---|---|---|---|
| **COOPERATIVE** (Positive State) | Caring Sensitive Nurturing Harmonizing Feeling-oriented | Logical Structured Organized Systematic Thinking-oriented | Spontaneous Creativity Playful Enthusiastic Action-oriented | Quiet Imaginative Insightful Reflective Inaction-oriented |
| **RELUCTANT** (Stress Responses) | Overadaptive Overpleasing Makes mistakes Cries Giggles Self-defeating Depressed | Overcritical Overworks Perfectionist Verbally attacks Demanding Complaining Take charge | Disruptive Blames Irresponsible Demands attention Defiant Breaking rules Physically aggressive | Disengaging Withdrawn Delays Despondent Daydreams Indecisive Silent treatment |

Depending on your personality, you have a tendency to be stressed by specific things and respond to stressors in different ways. Stress can be defined as any stimulus that interferes with normal equilibrium and can produce physical, mental or emotional tension. Stress can be a positive motivational force but too much stress can become disruptive to a person's life and health.

**TEACHER SCENERIOS**

The following teacher profiles highlight some predictable responses from teachers in both positive and stressful moments. Which one do you identify with?

### *Harmony*

Bob's response on the "Array Interaction Survey" indicates he rates high in the Harmony Personal Objective. When in a normal state (cooperative), he is caring and pro-social. His relationships with his students, and with family and friends, are important to him. He enjoys the school community and feels privileged to be impacting the lives of his students.

When highly stressed, Bob tends to over-adapt, over-please and make mistakes on the most routine items. Bob tends to be stressed by large amounts of paperwork, lack of social time with colleagues and not enough time to have one-on-one interactions with students. He may procrastinate, waste time by socializing and then feel badly because he doesn't have time for family, friends, or tasks that must be completed. He has a poor filing system, which expounds his paper dilemma. He also has a difficult time saying "no" and frequently finds himself on numerous committees and planning teams with a schedule that is overwhelming.

245

### *Production*

Mia's survey indicates she has a Production Personal Objective. She is logical, structured, organized and persistent. She is a thinker, a problem solver, likes information exchange and values such things as using time efficiently, task completion, skill development and schedules. Mia has many ideas and enjoys sharing them with colleagues. She is efficient, and her desk, lesson plans and materials are always well organized She is most likely to become stressed by changes in scheduling, too many unnecessary meetings, and confusing job descriptions, interruptions, or lack of specific information.

When Mia is stressed, she may become critical of herself and others. She may verbally disagree with a colleague's actions. She may put undue pressure on herself to do things perfectly, even neglecting to eat in order to finish a task. She tends to become curt when colleagues "waste her time" by engaging in frivolous chatter when she knows she could be accomplishing other more relevant tasks with her valuable time.

246

### Connection

Billie rated herself as having a Connection Personal Objective. She loves activity and action and enters a room with energy. She is friendly and bright eyed, connects with others in positive ways, enjoys music and drama and is very creative. She likes to try new things and never teaches the same material the same way twice. She enjoys the spontaneous moment.

When stressed, Billie can become irresponsible, disruptive, attention-getting and blaming. Her jokes may become inappropriate and sarcastic. She can become openly defiant to authority. Billie is stressed by high levels of structure, and when there is no room for creative thought or spontaneity in her planning or teaching, she stresses with relentless meetings, inflexible time schedules, and too much paperwork.

### Status Quo

Jose's survey results identify Status Quo as his Personal Objective. Jose is very quiet and reserved, insightful and reflective. When he speaks, both colleagues and students listen. He is good at repetitive tasks and enjoys putting lessons together on the computer and finding out additional information and activities from resources on the Internet.

When Jose becomes stressed, he begins to withdraw. He may lack enthusiasm and demonstrates little effort. He allows the students to do their own thing and does not pull it all back together for closure. He may sit at his desk to grade papers and find that 20 minutes has elapsed as he has been in a blank stare. Jose is most likely to be stressed by lack of specific direction and insufficient information. He is also stressed by too much activity with no break time for regrouping his thoughts and feelings. He tends to waste time by withdrawing and becoming indecisive.

**Section C**

# IDENTIFYING AND MODIFYING STRESS

## ENERGY DRAINS

Stress drains your energy, lowers your personal motivation, and frequently hinders your ability to solve problems and meet daily challenges. It is important to specify stressors so that you can avoid them, adjust to them and/or redirect your behavior. Learning how to deal with your stressors and subsequent energy drains are essential. The following examples follow Bob, Mia, Billie and Jose as they learn to manage their stress.

**Bob** - Stressors: *Too much paperwork -- too little socializing*
As soon as school is dismissed for the day, Bob is going to generate a list of the things he needs to accomplish before the next school day and prioritize the list. He is going to allow himself a 10-minute break to socialize and get a snack before returning to his classroom to implement the plan.

**Mia** - Stressors: *Too tightly scheduled -- poor nutrition*
Mia is going to allow 20 minutes in her schedule to adjust for any unscheduled time demands. She will pack a nutritious snack for mid-morning recess so that her physical energy is rejuvenated even before mid-day.

**Billie** - Stressors: *Rigid scheduling -- no fun time*
Billie is going to block out a time during the day where she and the class can choose to do something fun. She uses her creativity to generate a packet of learning games and activities.

**Jose** - Stressors: *Much activity and multi-tasking – no planning time*
Jose will stay in his room occasionally during lunch to give himself a chance to regroup for the rest of the day.

## PROACTIVE PLANNING

Identify constructive ways to manage your stress. Begin by thinking about activities or responsibilities that lead to energy drains and initiate stress responses. Consider specific actions to reduce the other "energy drains." The following sections will provide the next steps in your proactive plan, which include identifying your needs and building on the things that generate positive energy.

| **Energy Drains**<br>List what drains your energy | **Proactive Plan**<br>Ideas to reduce or eliminate energy drain |
| --- | --- |
| | |
| | |
| | |
| | |

*Our needs vary.*
*Sharing concerns and ideas with a colleague may be stress-relieving for some teachers but stressful for others.*

## IDENTIFYING NEEDS

In the last sections you considered --

- ❖ Your primary and secondary personality components (Personal Objectives).

- ❖ What activities/responsibilities stress you.

- ❖ How you personally respond to stress.

- ❖ Ways to proactively manage your stress.

When you consider your personality, it is important to understand what you need in order to stay in a positive and cooperative mode of interaction. It is important to know yourself and proactively plan ways to accommodate for your own psychological needs.

Bob, Mia, Billie and Jose identify specific ways their personality needs are met within the classroom context.

**Bob (Harmony)** values reciprocal friendship and needs a comforting work environment that is aesthetically pleasing to him.

**Mia (Production)** values accomplishment and needs to feel appreciated for her work efforts. Mia also needs a highly structured work environment.

**Billie (Connection)** values activity and needs to experience fun in her work environment. She needs to be involved in stimulating activity.

**Jose (Status Quo)** values privacy and stability. He needs quiet time in the day to think and prepare. Jose also needs predictable routines and schedules.

*If you fulfill your own needs,*
*you will be better able to balance your personal and professional life.*

## *Needs Chart*

The following chart shows the primary needs associated with each personality part and some possible ideas for ways to meet those needs.

| Personal Objective | Harmony | Production | Connection | Status Quo |
|---|---|---|---|---|
| **Psychological needs** | • Values self/others<br>• Sensory experiences | • Value for work<br>• Time schedule | • Values action<br>• Fun activity | • Values time<br>• Stability |
| **Ways to meet need** | • Value feelings<br>• Comfortable surroundings<br>• Personal effects (family photos, etc.)<br>• Time with friends | • Value ideas<br>• Incentives<br>• To-do list<br>• Routine for the day<br>• Organization | • Value activity<br>• Time for fun<br>• Hands-on activities<br>• Group interaction<br>• Change in routine<br>• Surprises | • Value quietness<br>• Independent activities<br>• Time for hobby<br>• Computer activities<br>• Routine tasks |

First identify your primary psychological needs. Then identify specific actions or activities that would fulfill these needs. List them below.

| My Primary Needs | Actions to Take |
|---|---|
|  |  |
|  |  |
|  |  |
|  |  |

**BUILDING ENERGY GAINS**

When your psychological needs are met, you actually feel confident, stronger and more capable; in other words, you actually gain energy.

On the chart below, write down actions or activities that energize you. Think of ways you can build these "Energy Gains" into your life.

Let's refer to our four example teachers:

- ❖ Writing a to-do list makes Mia feel accomplished and in control of her time.
- ❖ Jose goes for a quiet walk around the playground after school.
- ❖ Bob socializes with colleagues for 20 minutes after school.
- ❖ Billie puts on rock-n-roll and dances her way through class preparation.

| **Energy Gains**<br><br>List what energizes you | **Productive Plan**<br><br>Ideas to meet my needs |
|---|---|
|  |  |
|  |  |
|  |  |
|  |  |

*Take time to rest and relax!*

253

## WARNING SIGNS

As mentioned previously, teaching is rewarding, challenging, and fulfilling, but at the same time it is demanding, energy-draining and time-consuming. Becoming a teacher, just like being a newcomer in any other professional career, will require many adjustments. New faces, new responsibilities, new surrounding . . . all of these things together will often cause a sense of being "stressed." However, too much stress can cause physical problems. If you are experiencing any of the following symptoms, or a combination of these symptoms, it is important that you seek a doctor's attention. Mental/physical stress symptoms are your body's way of telling you to take it easy and put balance into your life. Remember, a well-balanced teacher can productively embrace each new day. Symptoms frequently associated with severe stress include:

❖ Recurring headaches

❖ Laryngitis

❖ Stomach problems

❖ Frequent heartburn

❖ Hostile feelings/language

❖ Depression/crying

❖ Sudden weight changes

❖ Tense back/neck muscles

❖ Unrelenting exhaustion

*You can only juggle and spin for a short period of time before it all comes crashing down.*

**STRESS RELIEVERS**

Use the following stress relievers to gain positive energy.

1. Stand up and do stretching exercises.
2. Close your eyes and think of a color; then picture five objects of that color.
3. Close your eyes and visualize your greatest achievement.
4. Crumple up a piece of paper and play "basketball" using your trashcan.
5. Drink a glass of water with small sips.
6. List five things you have enjoyed in the last month.
7. List five things you would like to do in the next month.
8. Think of some funny event from your life.   Laugh out loud.
9. Color a picture in a coloring book.
10. Take three deep, slow breaths in and out.

 Managing Time:

❖  Plan each day before it begins.
❖  Prepare for tomorrow's lessons tonight.
❖  Sort important tasks from less critical activities.
❖  Develop routines for managing repetitive tasks.
❖  Delegate; use student or parent helpers.
❖  Take care of your health.

*Trade Secrets*

**NOTES:**

**Section D**

# KEEPING IT ALL TOGETHER

## MANAGING THE PAPER AVALANCHE

Managing paper that awaits all teachers is a real challenge. This section provides suggestions that will help you manage your time and materials.

*"No one ever told me about the paperwork!"*

**Managing Time** - Schedule your time into two separate areas: School and home. When teachers get into the habit of taking school work home, they often begin to feel "overwhelmed" with teaching. No wonder teachers often feel that teaching is a 24-hour-a-day job! It is also important to learn how to make the most of your time at school.

**Calendar** - Purchase a calendar (the "month at a glance" type). Record school and personal activities immediately and update daily. Carry your calendar with you. Get in the habit of blocking out scheduled personal and family time. Only use one calendar.

**Mail** - Read through mail/memos at the end of the day. Throw away junk mail. Record important dates and deadlines on your calendar immediately, then throw the actual notice away. File important documents and respond to any requests immediately.

**After School** - Establish an efficient after-school routine. Save time by knowing what needs to be done and then do it.

## CREATING A COMFORTABLE WORK ENVIRONMENT

❖ Bring a small, electric, hot water pot to school so you can make coffee, tea, hot cocoa or soup during your breaks or after school. Check district policy first!

❖ Keep a supply of high protein/carbohydrate snacks to consume when your energy level runs low.

❖ Bring a radio/tape/CD player. Enjoy listening to your favorite music when you are planning your lessons.

❖ Bring an extra sweater, umbrella and a pair of comfortable shoes to keep in your closet or desk drawer. You never know when you might need extra comfort or warmth.

❖ Hang a mirror in your room. Keep extra grooming supplies in your desk.

❖ Bring tissues and first aid supplies.

*Make your desk a comfortable place to work.*

**CHAPTER CHECKLIST**

Do I...

Yes    No

☐    ☐    Know my primary and secondary personality/Personal Objectives?

☐    ☐    Know what things are most likely to trigger my stress?

☐    ☐    Know the ways I am most likely to respond to stress?

☐    ☐    Know my "Energy Drains"?

☐    ☐    Have a plan for combating those "Drains"?

☐    ☐    Know my psychological needs?

☐    ☐    Know some "Energy Gains"?

☐    ☐    Have plans for how I will address my own needs?

☐    ☐    Plan to take care of myself to stay positive?

☐    ☐    Have a comfortable work environment?

☐    ☐    Have a plan to manage paperwork?

*Trade Secrets*

**Notes:**

Chapter 9

# PREPARING FOR THE SUBSTITUTE TEACHER

**Even the most dedicated teachers will need a substitute one day.**

## HOW TO FACILITATE FOR THE SUBSTITUTE TEACHER

### SUBSTITUTE FOLDER

Even if you have "not had a cold in years," the likelihood of teachers needing the services of a substitute teacher is very high. It takes time to build your natural immunities. Therefore, it is strongly recommended that you organize a substitute folder. The purpose of developing this folder is to assist the substitute teacher in providing a coherent, quality educational experience during your absence.

A simple way to organize a substitute folder is to label a folder or a three-ring binder to hold lists and memos pertinent to your daily routine. Inside the folder, include the following:

**Lists:**

1. Seating chart/s.
2. School schedule.
3. Outline of your daily schedule.
4. Special classes, times and students affected.
5. List of ability/interest groups.
6. Names of students who are helpful.
7. Names of students who need special attention.
8. Names of helpful teachers (including aide and resource teachers).
9. List of parent volunteers (names, days, times).
10. List of how students are transported.

**Procedures:**

- ❖ Details regarding your welcoming/opening routines.
- ❖ Directions concerning your attendance procedure.
- ❖ Details concerning your management/discipline system.
- ❖ Information concerning specific instructional procedures.
- ❖ Restroom routines.
- ❖ Details regarding any duties you are assigned.

**Directions:**

- ❖ Location of supplies and instructional material.
- ❖ School map.
- ❖ Location of special classes.
- ❖ Location of teachers' workroom/restroom.

**Emergency Procedures:**

- ❖ Directions for fire/bomb/earthquake drill.
- ❖ Disruptive behavior protocol.
- ❖ Severe weather/rainy day schedule.

**Forms:**

- ❖ Discipline referral.
- ❖ Hall pass.
- ❖ LRC (Learning Resource Center) pass.
- ❖ Nurse's office pass.
- ❖ Guidance office pass.

 Make copies of some of the relevant materials from your personalized planner (see Chapter 2).

| Who's who? | Name | Phone Extension |
|---|---|---|
| ❖ Principal | _____ | _____ |
| ❖ Assistant Principal | _____ | _____ |
| ❖ Guidance Counselor | _____ | _____ |
| ❖ Secretary | _____ | _____ |
| ❖ Nurse | _____ | _____ |
| ❖ Custodian | _____ | _____ |
| ❖ Teachers next door | _____ | _____ |

**Example of Substitute Folder**

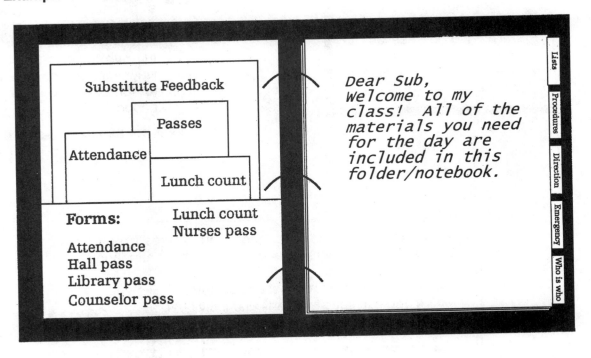

*The substitute folder helps you*
*be prepared for any unexpected situation.*

❖ Always remind your students that you expect them to demonstrate respect and appropriate behavior whenever a substitute teacher is present.

❖ Ask the substitute to evaluate your classroom. This technique holds your students accountable for their behavior when you are absent. The next page offers an example of the Substitute Teacher Evaluation form.

Many districts will ask you to evaluate the substitute teacher's performance. This information is used to determine who will be rehired to substitute at the school again. By that same token, the substitute may also be asked to evaluate your efforts to prepare for a substitute teacher.

At the end of each day, prepare for the possibility of a substitute the following day. Collect and organize teaching materials and place the sub folder on top. That way you are always ready for tomorrow, no matter what happens.

Districts have policies and procedures regarding substitute teachers. Read your district handbook to determine:

❖ Whom to call to request a substitute.
❖ If you can specify a particular individual.
❖ To whom substitute teachers report.

## FEEDBACK FOR THE TEACHER

Include a substitute teacher evaluation form in your notebook.  Example:

---

**Substitute Teacher Evaluation Form**

Substitute Teacher's Name _____ Date _____

Date: _____Phone # or Email_____

Overall evaluation of students' behavior:

    Disorderly/Rude                               Cooperative/Polite

   1      2      3      4      5      6      7      8      9      10

Individuals who were highly supportive/behaved appropriately:      Describe.

_____

_____

Individuals who were uncooperative/behaved inappropriately:      Describe.

_____

_____

Please list any assignments you were unable to complete:

_____

_____

Other comments:

_____

_____

Please include the homework you collected with this form.

Thank you.

---

*Trade Secrets*

**NOTES:**

268

**Section B**

# HOW TO BE A SUCCESSFUL SUBSTITUTE TEACHER

## SECURING A SUBSTITUTE POSITION

One way to establish yourself as an excellent teacher candidate is to work as a substitute teacher. To apply for a substitute teaching position, contact the district personnel office. Districts use similar hiring procedures to employ substitutes. (See "Teachers, How To Win the Job You Want," Enz & Kimerer, 2000.)

To increase your chances of being called to substitute, you may need to make contacts in numerous districts. Joining local teacher associations is one way to begin making connections. Another is to make an appointment to meet the principal or assistant principal at the schools where you wish to substitute (ask the secretary to make the appointment with whomever is in charge of coordinating substitutes). Before you meet with the appropriate administrator, it is wise to prepare yourself for the interview. Common interview questions may include:

- ❖ What is your teaching experience?

- ❖ Why do you want to substitute teach?

- ❖ What are your long-term career goals?

- ❖ Are you willing to substitute on any day of the week?

- ❖ What would you do if there were no lesson plans?

Also, think of questions that you may want to ask the interviewer:

- ❖ Does the school have a substitute training program?

- ❖ Are substitutes expected to attend faculty meetings?

- ❖ Do substitutes assume the extra duties that the teachers are assigned?

- ❖ What are the school's/district's discipline policies and procedures?

(Adapted from Manera, 1996)

269

When you meet with the appropriate administrator listen, question, and learn; bring your portfolio, and share your career goals. It will not be long before you receive calls to work as a substitute teacher.

## BEING AN EFFECTIVE SUBSTITUTE

The first rule of subbing is to be prepared!

❖ When you get "the call," it may be in the wee hours of the morning. Keep a memo pad and pencil by your phone. Find out as much as possible about the grade/subjects and school. Ask if you may call the teacher.

❖ Call the teacher if appropriate. Ask about the location of lesson plan book and any other pertinent information.

❖ Use the teacher's established classroom management system as much as possible.

❖ Use a briefcase or large bag/backpack to bring extra supplies/materials you may need. (See Teaching Tricks at the end of this chapter.)

❖ After school, go to the teachers' lounge and introduce yourself to the other teachers. Let them know you are interested in substituting for them in the future.

❖ Caution -- Do not share any negative details about the classrooms of teachers for whom you substitute, even if other teachers ask leading questions.

*Learning to work well with all faculty members is important.*

## MAINTAINING YOUR POSITION

To maintain your position you need to meet the expectations of administrators, teachers and students.

### Administrators want substitutes to:

❖ Arrive on time.

❖ Be in classrooms on time.

❖ Take accurate attendance.

❖ Maintain order.

❖ Willingly fulfill other duties as assigned (playground, bus duties).

### Teachers want substitutes to:

❖ Take attendance.

❖ Follow the provided lesson plans.

❖ Engage students in assigned activities and keep them on task.

❖ Maintain the physical order of the classroom.

### Students want the substitute to:

❖ Be able to teach the class and not baby sit.

❖ Introduce themselves and get a good start with students.

*Substitutes have many opportunities to learn about all ages and stages.*

(Adapted from St. Michel, 1994)

## LEARNING WHILE YOU SUBSTITUTE

Use the time you substitute as an opportunity to collect great teaching ideas.

- ❖ Bring a camera and take snapshots of creative bulletin boards.

- ❖ Bring a memo pad and write down examples of effective classroom management techniques.

- ❖ Make notes of interesting content-related activities.

- ❖ Talk to the teachers and ask more about the ideas you are able to collect.

## TEACHING TRICKS:  THE SUB BAG

Many classrooms are well equipped and organized. It is a joy to substitute for the classroom teacher. However, some classrooms are disorganized and may not be well stocked with everyday necessities. It is hard to predict; so to be adequately prepared, bring a substitute bag. The bag might include:

- ❖ Selection of books and short stories suitable for the grades you are teaching.

- ❖ Scissors, glue, ruler, tacks, rubber bands, note pads, small stapler and staples.

- ❖ Quick, easy activities you can use to become familiar with the students.

- ❖ Sponge activities that students complete as you are taking attendance.

- ❖ Supplemental games or activities to use if there is time left in the day or class period.

- ❖ Generic lesson plans -- primary and elementary.

- ❖ Blank transparencies and transparency pens.

- ❖ Selection of pencils, pens, markers and crayons.

- ❖ Blank paper, both unlined and lined.

- ❖ Money for lunch or bring your own lunch.

- ❖ Change for the soft-drink machine.

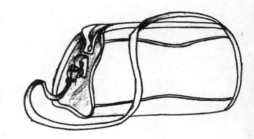

*"Have bag -- will teach."*

**CHAPTER CHECKLIST**

| Yes | No | |
|-----|-----|---|
| | | **How to Facilitate for the Substitute Teacher** |
| ☐ | ☐ | Have you developed a substitute folder/notebook? |
| ☐ | ☐ | Have you written a skeleton lesson plan? |
| ☐ | ☐ | Have you discussed appropriate "sub-behavior" with your students? |
| ☐ | ☐ | Have you developed a form to receive feedback from the substitute? |
| | | **How to Be a Successful Substitute Teacher** |
| ☐ | ☐ | Have you developed a "sub-bag"? |
| ☐ | ☐ | Have you organized a number of "all-purpose" activities? |
| ☐ | ☐ | Have you contacted a number of school districts? |

*Trade Secrets*

**NOTES:**

274

Chapter 10

# UNTIL THE LAST BELL RINGS

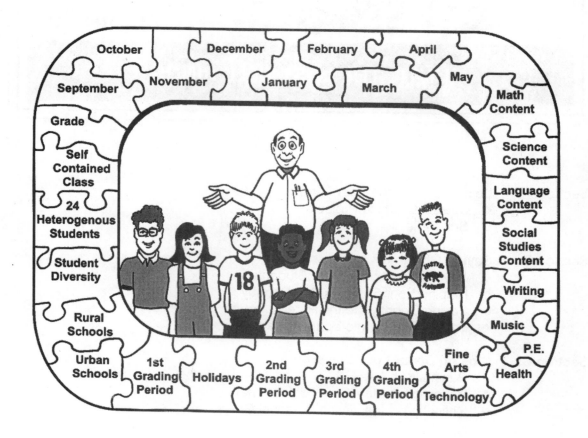

**Congratulations!!!** You have successfully put all the pieces together. Your class is well organized and your students are learning and well behaved. You are coming to the end of a very busy year. In many ways the end of the school year is as challenging as the start. There are dozens of details and administrative requirements that must be completed before summer vacation. You will quickly notice that even before this school year ends you begin to plan for the following year. This chapter reviews a number of concerns teachers have about ending the school year successfully, including how to keep your students engaged and learning until the last bell rings.

## Section A

## LEARNING UNTIL THE LAST MINUTE

At this time of year many students sense "the end is near" and often act accordingly. There is often a misperception that the end of the school year is not academically meaningful but only filled with "time-consuming" activities. However, you want to convey the message that the end of the school year is filled with rich opportunities for learning. This is also a time to engage the students in ways that they will:

- ❖ Acknowledge the classroom community.
- ❖ Celebrate their own personal abilities and talents.
- ❖ Consider ways they can learn throughout the summer.
- ❖ Look forward to coming back to school next year.

### SPECIAL LEARNING PROJECTS

In most states, standardized testing is completed in April. In many cases the required curriculum has been taught prior to state testing. Therefore, many expert teachers use this time to deliver high interest instructional projects that offer opportunities for children to apply all the skills they have learned. The following kindergarten teacher offers these suggestions:

*During May I teach a unit on* **WATER.** *Phoenix is extremely hot during the summer and many children have access to unsupervised pools. Hence, the drowning rate in this state is quite high. In this multi-faceted unit we talk about* **water safety** *rules and actually go to a community pool to practice swimming and life-saving procedures. Next, we learn about life in lakes, ponds and oceans. At this point we learn about the* **water ecosystems***. We turn our walls into a pond, a lake and the ocean. As the children learn about the special types of life at each level, they create and label each type of fish or water mammal. Finally, we learned about* **water conservation efforts** *and the* **water cycle***. We use this information to guide us as we plan our last day cleanup. We carefully recycle the water we use to clean our desks, counters and shelves. Then the children go outside to run through the sprinklers while the sprinklers water the grass.*

Notice that each activity in the WATER Unit was driven by academic content but also laced with many engaging activities. The children were learning and having fun learning until the last minute of kindergarten.

## SELF-REFLECTION

Children, like adults, need time to reflect upon the learning experiences they shared with you and their classmates. The following activities focus on summarizing the learning that students experienced and will hopefully store in their memories.

**Personal Scrapbook -** Have each student create a personal scrapbook of their year in your class.  The scrapbook is made with several pages of construction or butcher paper, and can be hole-punched and tied together with string or ribbon.  The student can include such items as:

- ❖ A list of the most important things they learned in class this year.
- ❖ Work from their portfolio or a drawing they have made.
- ❖ Snapshots you have taken of them engaged in classroom activities.
- ❖ Class pictures (you can make extra copies by using the copy machine).
- ❖ A page for the teacher to share something special about the student.

They may take this treasure home the last day of school.

**Top Ten List -** Have each student make a top ten list of their favorite memories, themes, projects, units of instruction and videos from this year.  They may personalize it in their own unique way.  The following is example written by a Tara, a third grader.

---

Dear Mrs. F.,

1. I love it when you read to us.  My favorite stories were from Mrs. Piggle-Wiggle.
2. I loved the "Coming to America" study.  I liked sharing my roots with the class.
3. I loved reading about Harriet Tubman and the Underground Railroad.
4. I loved our Signature T-Shirts.
5. I love DEAR.
6. I loved Brownie.
7. I even loved (sort of) the crayfish.
8. I love my best friends Sarah and Jessica.
9. I love that I'm going to 4th grade.
10. I will always love you.

---

 Try to keep classroom schedules, activities and routines the same for as long as possible. Students become confused and frustrated and misbehave when their lives are changed too frequently.

 Bring extra tissues.  The last day is usually more emotional than you expect.

**Timeline -** Ask each student to create a timeline representing each month of the school year. Ask them to identify special memories they have for each month. They may personalize this timeline in their own unique way. Hint: Some teachers conduct a memory brainstorm session before the students begin to write.

### *Terrel's Year*

September - Cursive writing. I wrote my Grandpa a letter before he died.

October - Fall Festival, my pumpkin won the face-carving contest.

November - Coming to America project – my mom videotaped me.

December - Collecting books and bears for poor kids.

January - Fractions and other hard math stuff.

February - Sending away a letter to the state that has my name on it.

March - Learning about Harriet Tubman.

April - Science Projects and TESTS.

May - Hobby Week.

***Keep routines and favorite activities intact as long as possible.***

**"All About ME" Letter** - Ask the children to write a letter to their next year's teacher. Ask them to tell this teacher what they like and do not like. They can include what they learned this year and what they want to learn next year.

---

Dear New Teacher

*What I Liked - I liked third grade because we learned a lot about science. We also had many animals in our class. Even though our first guinea pig named Buttons died we still got another named Brownie. I liked that my teacher read to us after lunch every day.*

*What I Don't Like - I don't like noisy classes, I don't like substitute teachers and I don't like the cafeteria salad bar.*

*What I Learned — I learned how to write in cursive, read chapter books, write a research project, do e-mails, fractions, multiply, and a whole lot more stuff.*

*What I Want to Learn - I want to learn to divide things, do web pages, a lot more science stuff.*

*Also - Could you read to us in 4th grade, too?*

*Love, Jerry*

---

 Reflection exercises not only help the students recall their learning experiences, they also allow the teacher to see what instructional activities children value most.

**Students enjoy remembering all the great activities they did with you.**

**Section B**

---

## SAYING GOODBYE

---

### SAYING GOODBYE TO YOUR STUDENTS

You have spent the better part of nine months with the students in your classroom. They have made an emotional impact on you and you have probably touched their lives in more ways than you'll ever know. Just as you planned their academic lessons every day it is now equally important for you to consider how you will plan to send them to the next grade level. Beyond their academic skills, you need to consider how you want them to feel about themselves as students and people. Saying goodbye to your students means you will need to consider:

❖ What memories you want them to have of their year with you.

❖ What learning legacies of themselves you want them to form.

**Making Memories -** Take a few moments and list three things you would like your students to think, believe or know after their year with you. These will become their memories of you and their learning legacy. Plan some specific ways you will embrace these into your end-of-year planning.

| What I want my students to think, believe and know: | Specific ways I will integrate this into my planning: |
|---|---|
| 1. _____ _____ | 1. _____ _____ |
| 2. _____ _____ | 2. _____ _____ |
| 3. _____ _____ | 3. _____ _____ |

The following page offers ideas to help develop the activities described on your list.

281

**Individual Conferences -** Take 3-5 minutes to share something very personalized and sincere with each student. Your comments may include your perceptions of their contributions to the classroom or an individual trait or ability you admire.

**Personal Letter -** Compose a letter or note to each student in your classroom. Describe your appreciation of the talents, qualities or contributions they have made to you, other students or the classroom during the year. Focus on the student's personal qualities, talents and gifts rather than on academic skills.

**Special Certificates -** Create an individualized "certificate" for each student. Each certificate is unique and highlights the students' special talents, qualities and characteristics. This certificate honors the student's characteristics and traits, not their accomplishment. Remember being awarded the "Most Improved" may be interpreted as a negative, not a positive. These certificates also help build pride and self-esteem. They help students feel capable and competent. The following list offers suggestions of personal qualities and special characteristics for you to consider.

### *Personal Traits and Special Qualities*

| | | |
|---|---|---|
| Risk-Taker | Cooperative | Dedicated |
| Artistic | Interdependent | Loyal |
| Inquisitive | Humorous | Committed |
| Diligent | Helpful | Critical Thinker |
| Persistent | Musical | Problem Solver |
| Respectful | Athletic | Self-Reliant |
| Compassionate | Optimistic | Courteous |
| Friendly | Awesome Attitude | Generous |
| Personable | Positive Thinker | Courageous |
| Outgoing | Honest | Polite |
| Confident | Caring | Gracious |
| Independent | Active Listener | Poised |

 This type of recognition is important and has a lasting effect. Teachers must always remember that each student is unique and has special gifts to share. Our job is to discover and celebrate these talents.

# HELPING YOUR STUDENTS SAY GOODBYE

During the past year the students in your class have formed bonds with one another. They have created a sense of classroom community that has many family-like features. As they leave this special sense of community, it is important for them to have opportunities to express their feelings. Next to the teacher's comments, students value what their peers say. The following ideas provide creative ways for students' to share the good things they feel about their friends and classmates.

**Group Graffiti -** Have a large poster or banner of butcher paper for the students to share written compliments to one another. Be sure everyone has something positive written about them by the end of the day. Sentence starter suggestions include:

- ❖ *"Thank you _____ for..."*
- ❖ *"I learned from_____ how to..."*
- ❖ *"_____ helped me to ..."*

**Center of the Circle -** Form a large circle and have students sit on the floor. Ask one to come to the center of the circle. Ask students to share, by raising their hand and waiting for you to call on them, their kind thoughts about the child in the center of the circle. The teacher may wish to model this initially. After the child in the center has heard five or six positive comments, ask the class to give them a hand. Repeat until each student has had an opportunity to be in the circle.

**T-Shirt Memories -** Have each student bring in an old T-shirt from home. Give each student a permanent marker. Have the students autograph one another's shirts. While they are signing their names, they must give one another a compliment.

The children will always remember th emotional warmth of these fond farewell for years.

The students will want to say thank you and goodbye to classroom aides and parent helpers. One idea would be to design a card for the person decorated and signed by all of the students.

## SAYING GOODBYE TO THE PARENTS

**Summary Letter -** Your students have learned so much during the school year. Many parents appreciate a summary letter to review the major academic units and learning achievements. To begin this summary it is helpful to review your long-term plans (see Chapter 1). You might wish to highlight academic units and special events from the student's perspectives. The following letter was co-written by Mrs. Jack's fourth grade class.

---

Dear Parents,

It has been a wonderful, busy and happy year for all the fourth graders in Mrs. Jack's class. We have learned so many things that we decided to brainstorm a list of our accomplishments month by month. Here are the results:

In September we learned about how our body functions. We studied the heart by making heart pumps to learn how they work. We visited the heart exhibit at the science museum. We also practiced complex multiplication.

In October we studied our lungs. We learned how smoking damages the lungs. A doctor from the hospital visited and actually showed us examples of healthy lungs and smokers' lungs. We began RAT (Read-A-Thon). If we read 1,000 hours altogether we will win a prize. We figured if we read for 30 minutes daily we would reach this goal.

In November and December we collected food for a family that needed help. With everyone's help we were able to give a special family of six a happy holiday. We also learned about how different families in our class celebrated the holidays. We had 300 hours towards RAT.

In January we learned about how America grew. We traced our family's roots to learn how we came to America. The families in our room came from Europe, Africa, South America, China and Polynesia. We charted this information on the map. We had read 500 RAT hours.

In February we learned about the origin of Valentine's Day. We also wrote valentines to the grandmas and grandpas at the senior citizen home. We visited them when we gave them our cards. We interviewed them and asked them where their families originated. We took that information and added it to the "Where in the World?" graph.

In March we studied fractions, fractions, fractions. We converted them, multiplied them, added, subtracted and equalized them. We had 800 RAT hours.

In April we took a number of tests. We think we did extremely well but we were glad when the tests were all done. RAT is now at 900!

It's May and we won our class prize for reading 1,000 hours during RAT. We all had a great year. We want to thank the parents for all their help.

Sincerely, Mrs. Jack's 4th (almost 5th) Grade Class

---

**Satisfaction Survey -** Towards the end of the spring semester, many schools routinely ask parents to complete a survey about their satisfaction with the curriculum, the school and the teacher. Often the teacher is asked to send the survey home with the students and then collect the information for the school administration to summarize. In some schools the survey is sent directly to the parents via the mail. In this situation the survey is accompanied by a postage-paid, direct return envelope.

However the data is collected, it is important for the parents to have an opportunity to give feedback to the teacher and the school. If your school does not collect this type of information, you may wish to develop a one-page questionnaire. For example:

Dear Parents,

I would like you to provide feedback regarding how well you believe your son/daughter did in _____ grade. For each question, please circle the number that reflects your views.

1 = Strongly Disagree   2 = Disagree   3 = Agree   4 = Strongly Agree

1. I believe my son/daughter accomplished the math objectives for _____.   1   2   3   4

2. I believe my son/daughter accomplished the reading objectives for _____.   1   2   3   4

3. I believe my son/daughter accomplished the writing objectives for _____.   1   2   3   4

4. I believe my son/daughter accomplished the science objectives for _____.   1   2   3   4

5. I believe my son/daughter accomplished the social studies objectives for _____.   1   2   3   4

6. I believe my son/daughter enjoyed learning this year in _____.   1   2   3   4

7. I believe my son/daughter enjoyed being part of this class.   1   2   3   4

8. I believe my son/daughter enjoys reading.   1   2   3   4

9. I believe my son/daughter enjoys math.   1   2   3   4

10. I believe my son/daughter enjoys writing.   1   2   3   4

11. I believe my son/daughter enjoys science.   1   2   3   4

12. I believe my son/daughter enjoys social studies.   1   2   3   4

13. I believe the teacher helped my son/daughter develop academically.   1   2   3   4

14. I believe my son/daughter's teacher helped my son/daughter develop socially.   1   2   3   4

15. Comments

**Recognition Tea** – The parents, like the students, have played an important part in your classroom community. Therefore, it is important to recognize their contributions. Many principals sponsor a school-wide, end-of-the-year celebration for parents who have volunteered in various ways throughout the year. In this case the school secretary will ask you for the names of the parents who have supported your classroom.

If the school does not sponsor the celebration, it a good idea to invite the parents to attend the end-of-the-year party. The students can help make special recognition cards. A heartfelt thank you is always appreciated.

**Summer Activities** – Teachers may wish to send home a Summer Activity Packet on the last day of school. The packet may include:

❖ Age-appropriate learning activities that parent's and children may complete together.
❖ A listing of local educational programs that are sponsored by the city, local university, YMCA, etc.
❖ A reminder of summer safety tips.

## SAYING GOODBYE TO YOUR COLLEAGUES

Though you will see most of your colleagues and administrators next year, it is a wise idea to compose thank you notes for people who have helped you throughout the year. These could include the principal, assistant principal, nurse, secretary, custodian and your grade-level teammates. While it takes a few minutes to write your appreciation, the recipients of your thanks will greatly appreciate them.

*You made many new collegial friendships this year. Be sure to say "Thank you!"*

## CLOSING DOWN YOUR CLASSROOM

**PUTTING IT ALL AWAY**

Do you remember the hours you spent at the beginning of the year setting up your classroom? Well, the good news is that it will take less time to take it down than it did to put it up. The bad news is that you will have much more to put away.

**Organizational Scheme -** As you put away teaching materials you will also need to consider how to organize your instructional units so that you may retrieve them easily next year. Some teachers use a subject-by-subject approach, while others use a month-by-month scheme. Teachers who use an integrated approach will store materials by thematic units.

 When you put materials away, use heavy plastic containers with snap-on lids (20-30 gallon size). Though the initial cost is more than cardboard boxes, the plastic containers are durable and do a better job of protecting teaching materials.

 Veteran teachers suggest leaving bulletin boards up until after primary children have left. Though it may take a day to complete this task, the children are more likely to behave better if their surroundings stay as constant as possible.

**Check-Out List -** In addition to organizing your teaching materials, you will need to accomplish a number of administrative tasks for the librarian, nurse, secretary and principal. Most schools provide a list of actions you must complete before the end of the school year. The following list provides examples of end-of-year responsibilities:

- ❖ Submit gradebooks with class rosters and attendance sheets.

- ❖ Insert grades onto a permanent file card for each individual student.

- ❖ Return all software and A.V. materials to the learning resource or media center.

- ❖ Return curriculum materials or teacher editions.

- ❖ Return textbooks, manipulatives and learning aids to designated storage area/s.

- ❖ Turn in textbook lists and requested purchase orders for next year.

- ❖ Turn in completed list of schedule preferences for next year's class schedule.

- ❖ Turn in recommendations for next year's student placements.

- ❖ Return all school-owned equipment/materials to designated areas for storage.

- ❖ Turn in completed supply requests and standard stock requisitions.

- ❖ Clear classroom walls.

- ❖ Return next year's contract to Human Resources.

- ❖ Provide district/school office with summer addresses and telephone numbers.

- ❖ Return all keys.

- ❖ Pick up paycheck/s from building administrator when entire list is complete.

## REFLECTIONS: IDENTIFYING PROFESSIONAL GOALS

The end of the school year is a perfect time to reflect upon the accomplishments of the past year. It is a time to consider:

❖ What you learned and what you still want to know.

❖ What you did well and what you want to do better.

The guided-reflection form will help you to review your year, celebrate your triumphs and establish new goals.

The outcome I am most pleased with from this year of teaching is…

The thing I am most disappointed about from this year is…

The part of teaching that is most natural for me is…

The part of teaching that is the most difficult for me is…

One thing that really helped me from my preservice or inservice training was…

The one thing that I could not have been prepared for, regardless of preparation…

The best part of teaching is…

## REFLECTIONS: IDENTIFYING PERSONAL GOALS

You have worked extremely hard this year to:

- ❖ Establish your classroom environment.
- ❖ Develop classroom community.
- ❖ Create interesting learning opportunities.
- ❖ Manage student behavior.
- ❖ Organize parent-teacher conference.
- ❖ Collect and document evidence of student learning, etc., etc., etc.

In other words, you are now a continuing teacher! In addition to considering your professional goals, it is time to consider your personal goals. Take a few moments to assess your personal desires.

The thing I missed doing the most this year was...

The non-school related thing I thought about doing the most this year was...

One health concern I have is...

One book I want to read or movie I want to see is...

One person I want to have a long conversation with is...

**CHAPTER CHECKLIST**

Yes   No

☐   ☐   Do you have special learning projects planned for closing down the year?

☐   ☐   Have you planned time and activities for meaningful reflection for your students?

☐   ☐   Have you planned specific ways to leave a legacy for what you want your students to think, know and believe after their year with you?

☐   ☐   Have you planned a way to celebrate each child in your classroom?

☐   ☐   Have you designed ways for your students to say goodbye to you, and their friends?

☐   ☐   Have you created a closing letter and/or way to say "thank you" to your students' parents?

☐   ☐   Do you have a plan for putting it all away?

☐   ☐   Have you taken time to reflect on your year and your accomplishments?

☐   ☐   Have you set goals for your summer and your next school year?

**Notes:**

## WORD TO THE WISE:
## TIPS FROM TEACHERS AND ADMINISTRATORS

Becoming a skilled and effective professional takes times and dedication. It also takes the process of experience. Following are some sets of tips for success in teaching given by teachers and administrators. Enjoy implementing the wisdom....

### TIPS FROM TEACHERS AND MENTORS

A group of first-year teachers and mentor teachers, participants in the Beginning Educator Support Team (BEST) program offered by Arizona State University to a number of school districts in the Phoenix metropolitan area, were asked to give a "word of wisdom" or advice for teachers. They offered the following:

#### *On Discipline*

- ❖ Set a clear discipline plan at the beginning and stick to it.
- ❖ Be consistent with your rules, consequences and procedures.
- ❖ Be fair and treat all students the same.
- ❖ Include students in the making of the classroom management rules.
- ❖ Always think positive -- tomorrow will be better.
- ❖ Positive reinforcement, positive reinforcement, positive reinforcement. Students flourish and strive to please their teacher when they receive positive feedback; this keeps discipline problems to a minimum.
- ❖ Be prepared. Planning affects discipline. If every minute is filled, then interest is generated and problems are lessened.
- ❖ Document the various strategies you have tried for a child with a behavior problem. When you need to gain administrative support, this will help your administrator support you more specifically.

### *On Lesson Planning*

❖ PLAN, PLAN, PLAN, but be flexible and ready to improvise as well.
❖ Try to plan ahead. Have your lesson plans ready before class time and Rehearse, Rehearse, Rehearse.
❖ Do not try to teach too many things at once. Set one goal at a time and move on after your goal was accomplished.

### *On Organization*

❖ Be organized, but do not stress if things are a mess or if things are not finished, because this is teaching!
❖ Get to your school a week ahead of time if this is possible. It will save you a lot of heartache during the first days of school.
❖ Allow plenty of time before school starts to get "set up."
❖ Make "to do" lists and prioritize.

*Everyone feels overwhelmed at first.*

### On Relationships with Parents, Colleagues, and Students

* ❖ Introduce yourself to parents and talk to them before problems develop.
* ❖ Send newsletters and make happy phone calls too.
* ❖ Be open to and welcome parent involvement.
* ❖ Work close with a veteran/mentor teacher. Ask questions for help.
* ❖ Talk with other teachers and get ideas and information from them.
* ❖ Smile, be friendly and force yourself to socialize with your colleagues (even when you are not in the mood). Do not isolate yourself.
* ❖ Get to know the secretaries and your custodian. They both know a lot of things about your school, and the custodian may be able to get you things you need.
* ❖ Don't gossip.
* ❖ Talk to your students. Get to know them, build a relationship of trust and learning will blossom.
* ❖ Tell your students you are proud of them.

**Becoming part of the team takes time and effort.**

## *On Taking Care of Yourself*

❖ Be yourself. Do not try to be someone else.

❖ Teaching takes a lot of energy.  Eat well and get plenty of sleep.

❖ Have a separate life of your own.  Make time for yourself and do not let teaching become your only life.  Be an interesting person involved in many aspects of life and bring that enthusiasm to your students.

❖ Relax and do not over-absorb yourself.

❖ Forgive each day!  Start each day fresh. Remember that you have the rest of the school days to correct what you did wrong today.

❖ Get help immediately when needed.

❖ Have faith that eventually it all falls into place and makes sense.

❖ Remember to laugh and enjoy the beauty of children.

❖ Yes, teaching is extremely frustrating at times, and it is very easy to feel alone -- but you are not.

❖ Accept that some problems have no answers.

❖ You cannot solve and do everything all by yourself.

❖ Always do your best and feel great about it!

❖ Whatever you do, do not let your expectations and your feelings of being overwhelmed keep you from doing your job.  Just get in there and do it.  If it does not work, then you know that you need to do or try something else.

❖ When you are sick, STAY HOME!

❖ Prepare for a sub before you need one.

**Rest, take your shoes off and take time for yourself.**

## TIPS FROM ADMINISTRATORS

- ❖ Prepare thoroughly for first day and first week of school.
- ❖ Ask for a mentor and get to know this support person.
- ❖ Obtain curriculum materials.
- ❖ Meet with your department chair/grade level leader for advice and direction.
- ❖ Know school leader/s expectations of you. Meet with your evaluator for clarification.
- ❖ Volunteer to assist in your area/s of expertise as committees and extra-curricular activities are assigned.
- ❖ Create your management plan, both proactive and corrective. Learn special daily procedural expectations for the first week of school. Such as student enrollment counts and lunch counts.
- ❖ Ask questions if you are unclear about your responsibilities.

### *Advice from an Administrator to a Beginning Educator*

Dear First-Year Teacher,

Your first year of teaching is one of the most exciting times of your life. It is the reward for all of the hard work that you put in to prepare yourself for this role. You finally have a class that is all your own!

Now you have the opportunity to practice all that you learned. What you will find out is that situations will arise that nothing you have learned will prepare you for. You will need to make good judgments, seek support from veteran educators and administration, and learn from your experiences.

If I could emphasize one piece of advice, it is to concentrate on classroom management. Build your skills one day at a time. Soon you will develop the wealth of application you admire in a master teacher.

I encourage you to find a mentor if you don't already have one assigned. Use this person to discuss your challenges as well as your successes. Sometimes just talking things through with someone who has experience is all that you need.

Communicating with parents on a regular basis will add to your success. Call them about both the positive and the negative. Build trust. It will prevent so many problems in the long run if you take the time to establish this communication!

Education is the most rewarding profession there is! You can and do make a difference!

Sincerely,

Veteran Administrator

**Veteran's View:**

It takes time to make a difference in the political aspects of the school and community. Focus on making a difference with students before you assume the role of "revamping" the system.

**Principal's Principles:**

It takes special skill to work effectively with a paraprofessional. Think and talk about collaboration and team building with instructional assistants who may be assigned to you.

**Mentor's Moments:**

Celebrate the little successes... they add up to big victories.

**Coach's Corner:**

Establish and maintain a support system. Include your family, your new colleagues, friends, and your peers with whom you established a network throughout your teacher preparation program. Isolation is the number one enemy of teachers!

## Notes:

# Notes:

# REFERENCES

(References listed are in text and other references
were also included for additional information.)

Algozzine, B., Ysseldyke, J., & Elliot, J. (1997). *Strategies and Tactics for Effective Instruction*. Longmont, CO: Sopris West.

Arends, R.I. (1994). *Learning to Teach*. New York: McGraw Hill, Inc.

Becker, H., & Epstein, J. (1982). Parent involvement: A study of teacher practices. *Elementary School Journal*, 83(2), 85-102.

Bradley, D.F., King-Sears, M.E., & Tessier-Swititlick, D.M. (1997). *Educating Students in Inclusive Settings*. Boston, MA: Allyn & Bacon.

Brooke, D.M., & Hawke, G. (1985). Effective and ineffective session opening: Teacher activity and task structures. Paper presented at the American Educational Research Association, Chicago.

Carlson, A.C. (1990). *Family Questions*. New Brunswick, NJ: Transaction.

Cawthorne, B. (1987). *Instant Success for New and Substitute Teachers*. Scottsdale, AZ: Greenfield Publications.

Charles, C.M. (1992). *Building Classroom Discipline* (4th edition). White Plains, NY: Longman Publishing Company.

Christie, J., Enz, B., & Vukelich, C. (2002). *Teaching Language and Literacy: Preschool Through the Elementary Grades* (2nd Edition). New York, NY: Addison, Wesley, Longman Publishing Company.

Collins, Cathy. (1987) *Time Management for Teachers: Practical Techniques and Skills That Give You More Time To Teacher*. Parker Publishing Company.

Cruickshank, D.R., Bainer, D., & Metcalf, K. (1995). *The Act of Teaching*. New York: McGraw Hill.

Dreikurs, R., & Cassel, P. (1972). *Discipline Without Tears: What to Do with Children Who Misbehave*. New York: Hawthorne Books.

Dyck, N., Pemberton, J., Woods, K., & Sundbye, N. (1996). *Creating Inclusive Schools -- A New Design for All Students*. Lawrence, KS: Curriculum Solutions, Inc.

Edwards, C.H. (1997). *Classroom Discipline & Management.* Columbus, Ohio: Merrill.

Emmer, C., & Evertson, C. (1981). Synthesis of research on classroom management. *Educational Research*, 38(4), 341-347.

Emmer, C., & Evertson, C. (1980). Effective management at the beginning of the school year in junior high classes. Research and Development Center for Teacher Education, The University of Texas, Austin.

Emmer, E.T., et al. (1989). *Classroom Management for Secondary Teachers* (2nd edition). Englewood, NJ: Prentice-Hall.

Enk, J., & Hendricks, M. (1981). *Shortcuts For Teachers: Strategies for Reducing Classroom Workload.* Pitman Learning, Inc.

Enz, B., & Kimerer, K. (2000). *Teachers - How To Win the Job You Want.* Dubuque, Iowa: Kendall-Hunt Publishers.

Epstein, J. (1986). Parent's reactions to teacher practices of parent involvement. *Elementary School Journal*, 86(3), 277-294.

Evertson, C.M., Emmer, E.T., Clements, B.S., Sanford, J.P., & Worsham, M.E. (1984). *Classroom Management for Elementary Teachers.* Englewood Cliffs, NJ: Prentice-Hall.

Field, M.V., Spangler, K.L., & Lee, D.M. (1991). *Let's Begin Reading Right: Developmentally Appropriate Beginning Literacy.* New York, NY: Merrill-Macmillan Publishing Company.

Flaxman, E., & Inger, M. (1991). Parents and schooling in the 1990s. *ERIC Review*, 1(3), 2-5.

Fredericks, A.D., & Rasinski, T.V. (1990). Involving the uninvolved: How to. *The Reading Teacher*, 43, 424-425.

Freericks, C.A. (1996). Classroom management and student discipline: A workshops series. Tempe, Arizona: Arizona State University.

Gelfer, J.I. (1991). Teacher-parent partnerships - Enhancing communications. *Childhood Education*, 67, 164-167.

Giangreco, M.R., Colinger, C.J., & Iverson, V.S. (1993). *Choosing Options and Accommodations for Children.* Baltimore, MD: Paul Brookes.

Glasser, W. (1986). *Control Theory in the Classroom.* New York: Harper & Row.

Gordon, T. (1974). *T.E.T.: Teacher Effectiveness Training*. New York: Peter H. Wyden.

Hammeken, P.A. (1995). *450 Strategies for Success - A Practical Guide for All Educators Who Teach Students with Disabilities*. Minnetonka, MN: Peytral Publications.

Harrison, A., & Burton Spuler, F. (1983*). Hot Tips for Teachers: A Collection of Classroom Management Ideas*. David S. Lake Publishers.

Hawley, C. (1995). *Icebreakers*. Ttalk@indiana.edu. World Wide Web.

Hines, R.A., & Johnston, J.H. (1996). Inclusive classrooms: The principal's role in promoting achievement. National Association of Secondary School Principals.

Jones, V.F., & Jones, L.S. (1995). *Comprehensive Classroom Management: Creating Positive Learning Environments for All Students* (4th ed.). Needham Heights, MA: Allyn & Bacon.

Knaupp, J. (1995). *Array Model*. Unpublished document. College of Education, Arizona State University, Tempe, AZ.

Kortman, S. (1997). I know me: Personal objective response sheet. College of Education, Arizona State University, Tempe, AZ.

Kounin, J. (1970). *Discipline and Groups Management in Classrooms*. New York: Holt, Rinehart and Winston.

Kronowitz, E.L. (1992). *Your First Year of Teaching and Beyond* (2nd ed.). New York: Longman.

Lipsky, D.K., & Gartner, A. (1997). *Inclusion and School Reform*. Baltimore, MD: Paul H. Brookes Publishing.

Londergan, G. (1988). Helping parents understand the stages of their child's reading development. *ERIC Clearinghouse on Reading and Communication Skills*, #101.

Lovitt, T.C. (1997). *Special Education*. Longmont, CO: Sopris West.

Manera, E. (1996). *Substitute Teaching: Planning for Success*. West Lafayette, IN: Kappa Delta Pi Publications.

McCoy, M.K. (1995). *Teaching Special Learners in the General Education Classroom*. Denver, CO: Love Publishing Company.

McLaughlin, B. (1992). Myths and misconceptions about second language learning: What every teacher needs to unlearn. *National Center for Research on Cultural Diversity and Second Language Learning*, 1-9.

Montgomery, J.K. (1996). Selected strategies for inclusive classrooms. In Florian L. and Rouse, M. (Eds.). *School Reform and Special Educational Needs: Anglo-American Perspectives.* Cambridge, MA: University of Cambridge Institute of Education.

Moore, E. (1991). Improving schools through parental involvement. *Principal,* 71(1), 17, 19-20.

Ottlinger, K., & Kohlhepp, P. (1992). Curricular adaptations: Accommodating the instructional needs of diverse learners in the context of general education. Kansas State Board of Education.

Pugach, M.C., & Warger, C.L. (Eds.) (1996). *Curriculum Trends, Special Education, and Reform: Refocusing the Conversation.* New York: Teachers College Press.

Putnam, J.K. (Ed.). (1993). *Cooperative Learning and Strategies for Inclusion: Celebrating Diversity in the Classroom.* Baltimore, MD: Paul H. Brookes.

Quest International. (1991). *Energizers and Other Great Cooperative Activities For All Ages.* Written and compiled by Carol Apacki. Quest Books.

Quinton, D., & Rutter, M. (1988). *Parenting Breakdown. The Making and Breaking of Inter-Generational Links.* Aldershot, England: Avebury.

Rennie, J. (1993). ESL and bilingual models. *ERIC Clearinghouse on Language and Linguistics.*

Roland, R. (November 1976). Discipline with dignity. *Early Years.*

Sanford, J., & Evertson, C. (1980). Beginning the school year at a low SES junior high. Austin, TX: Research and Development Center for Teacher Education.

Skrtic, T.M. (Ed.) (1995). *Disability and Democracy: Reconstructing (Special) Education for Postmodernity.* New York: Teachers College Press.

Slavin, R.E. (1995). *Cooperating Learning.* Needham Heights, MA: Allyn & Bacon.

St. Michel, T. (1994). Substitute teachers: Who? What? How? When? Where? Why? A case study of the substitute process. Unpublished doctoral dissertation, Arizona State University, Tempe, AZ.

Stainback, S., & Stainback, W. (1992). *Curriculum Considerations in Inclusive Classrooms.* Baltimore, MD: Paul H. Brookes Publishing.

Stainback, S., & Stainback, W. (1996). *Inclusion: A Guide for Educators*. Baltimore, MD: Paul H. Brookes Publishing.

Tauber, R.T. (1995). *Classroom Management: Theory and Practice* (2nd ed.). New York: Harcourt Brace.

Turnbull, A.P., & Turnbull, H.R.III. (1997). *Families, Professionals, and Exceptionality: A Special Partnership* (3rd ed.). Upper Saddle River, NJ: Merrill/Prentice Hall.

U.S. Department of Education. (1995). The seventeenth annual report to Congress on the Individuals with Disabilities Education Act. Washington, DC.

Vaughn, S., Box, C.S., & Schumm, J.S. (1997). *Teaching Mainstreamed, Diverse, and At-Risk Students in the General Education*. Boston, MA: Allyn & Bacon.

Villa, R., & Thousand, J. (1997). The inclusion puzzle: Putting the pieces together. Paper presented at the annual convention of the Council for Exceptional Children, Salt Lake City, UT.

Warner, J., Bryan, C., & Warner, D. (1995). *The Unauthorized Teacher's Survival Guide*. IN: Park Avenue Publications.

Williamson, B. (1988). *A First Year Teacher's Guide for Success: A Step-by-Step Educational Recipe Book*. Sacramento, CA: Dynamic Teaching Company.

Willis, S. (1994). Teaching language-minority students: Role of native-language instruction is debated. *ASCD Update, 36(5), 1, 4-5.*

Winebrenner, S. (1992). *Teaching Gifted Kids in the Regular Classroom*. Minneapolis, MN: Free Spirit Publishing, Inc.

Wolfgang, C.H. (1995). *Solving Discipline Problems: Methods and Models for Today's Teachers* (3rd ed.). Boston, MA: Allyn & Bacon.

Wong, H.K., & Wong, R.T. (1991). *The First Days of School - How to Be an Effective Teacher*. Sunnyvale, CA: Harry K. Wong Publications.